To: Ruth De Los Santos
Thanks for stopping by!
Onward Christian



# RETURN OF THE CHRISTIAN

## VOL I: THE STAND

John F. Feet

www.returnofthechristian.com

Xulon ELITE

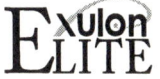

Copyright © 2015 by John F. Feet

*Return of the Christian*
*Vol I: The Stand*
by John F. Feet

Printed in the United States of America.

ISBN 9781498435918

All rights reserved solely by the author. The author guarantees all contents are original and do not infringe upon the legal rights of any other person or work. No part of this book may be reproduced in any form without the permission of the author. The views expressed in this book are not necessarily those of the publisher.

Unless otherwise indicated, Scripture quotations are taken from the New American Standard Bible (NASB). Copyright © 1960, 1962, 1963, 1968, 1971, 1972, 1973, 1975, 1977, 1995 by The Lockman Foundation. Used by permission. All rights reserved.

www.xulonpress.com

# Table of Contents

*Dedication* . . . . . . . . . . . . . . . . . . . . . . . . . . . . . . . . . . vii
*Acknowledgements* . . . . . . . . . . . . . . . . . . . . . . . . . . . . ix
*Note to the Reader* . . . . . . . . . . . . . . . . . . . . . . . . . . . . xi
*Introduction* . . . . . . . . . . . . . . . . . . . . . . . . . . . . . . . . xiii

Chapter 1:  First Things First . . . . . . . . . . . . . . . . . . . . 21
Chapter 2:  Politics and Religion: Oil and Water? . . 38
Chapter 3:  What Are We Afraid Of? . . . . . . . . . . . . . 68
Chapter 4:  From Whence We Came . . . . . . . . . . . . . 95
Chapter 5:  The Time For Action Has Come . . . . . . 115
Chapter 6:  Judgment or Discernment? –
            The Example of the Pharisees . . . . . . . . 138
Chapter 7:  The Hardened Heart . . . . . . . . . . . . . . . 166
Chapter 8:  …And God Gave Them Over . . . . . . . . 192
Chapter 9:  Put On The Full Armor Of God . . . . . . 223
Chapter 10: Girding Our Loins . . . . . . . . . . . . . . . . . 250

*Afterword:*  My Story and The Invitation
              of a Lifetime . . . . . . . . . . . . . . . . . . . . . 255

# Dedication

This work is dedicated to Dr. Mark Liederbach who taught me two very important lessons: death to sin is both a non-repeatable act and a daily commitment. And though he may not remember it, Mark also taught me how to dedicate a book with sincere humility and a thankful heart.

# Acknowledgements

This book was inspired by God and prodded forward by a poor suffering wife who, on more than one occasion, scolded her husband by declaring to exhaustion, "Don't tell me, tell them!" My wife, Rita, a graduate with a Master of Divinity in Women's Studies from Southeastern Baptist Theological Seminary, also provided a unique perspective on the specific issues Christian women face in taking a stand for Christ. She is my ruby (Proverbs 31:10), and after 30 years of marriage, still causes my heart to leap like a gazelle with a single bat of her eyes.

Margot Bass, my editor, is truly a gift from God. Every author struggles when it comes to putting his work under the knife. Margot is a skilled surgeon whose spiritual gift has blossomed into an amazing asset. Although I have been blessed with her talents all to myself, it will not be long before she is in great demand.

Yet this book would not have gone to print, were it not for the entire committed team at Xulon Press. They took a chance on an unknown author, threw all of their publishing might behind this project and even beamed at the thought of undertaking a three-book series, again, by an unknown author. I will most likely end up at the kiddies' table at the Lord's Great Banquet, but I will occasionally glance over at the big table and rejoice with these folks as they reap the rewards for the risk they took.

Most importantly, I must thank you, the reader. Wherever you are in your walk with Christ, I know this book will strike a raw nerve. God has prepared us all for what lies ahead, and we will go through that fire together until that day we will rejoice together with Jesus, forever in His arms.

# Note to the Reader

This book is written, inspired by God's love, to Protestant and Catholic alike, as well as to "unbelievers"- those who have not yet, for their own private reasons, determined to live their life for Christ. I mean no disrespect by the term "unbeliever," and I would be the first to agree that some may infer a level of disdain from its use. I certainly, and most humbly, intend no such implication. I use the term as it is used biblically, to describe those who have exercised their own free will to determine their own destiny apart from Christ.

To the "unbelievers" who exercise their free will to pick up and read this little book, I can only thank you with all of my heart. If you are reading this and think this is only for Christians, I want you to know that you are both a major player in this book and the reason for its existence.

If you want to know my story, you can always skip to the Afterword at the end of this book. But with nothing but love in my heart for you, I challenge you to test your open-mindedness and first read this short book with an honest heart and a critical eye. You may bristle at times, but please be patient with me. I invite you to see what one Christian urges other Christians to do in the face of relentless adversity. Get an insider's view of how we plan to stand upon our faith. Not to chide you, but with all due respect, you have nothing to fear from what lies between these pages. If nothing else, you'll know what we're up to. We have no secrets from each other. I most humbly ask you to remember that every Christian alive today, in fact every Christian who has ever lived, was once an unbeliever. Therefore, no true Christian thinks more highly of himself than he does of the unbeliever.

# Introduction to *The Return of the Christian Series*

**There was a time…**

There was a time when "planned parenthood" described a husband and wife discussing how many children God would bestow upon them.

There was a time when adults refrained from swearing and uttering vulgarities in public, at least within earshot of our children.

There was a time when G-rated movies not only ruled the box office; they also relied on uplifting themes of redemption rather than countless gags on human flatulence.

There was a time when we didn't have to suffer through commercials rescuing us from the perils of erectile dysfunction, wholesale touting of birth control devices, and the inevitable admonishment of safe sex with same sex partners.

There was a time when parents had control over the curriculum in the public classroom, financed dearly by their own tax dollars rather than lotteries.

There was a time when boys and girls went unmolested in the grocery store checkout lane by sexually provocative magazine covers and raunchy tabloids stacked next to the candy bars.

There was a time when adults responsibly fulfilled their social obligation by tempering a misbehaving child in public, whether their own or someone else's.

There was a time when parents were held legally responsible for their child's actions.

There was a time when our children did not have immediate and unfettered electronic access to pornographic content, so outrageous and deviant, that even Hugh Hefner wouldn't publish it.

There was a time in primetime television when parents did not have to worry about storylines on masturbation, teen sex, sexually charged serial killers, homosexual aggrandizement and adulterous housewives.

There was a time when we never had to question if the school bus driver was high on legally consumed marijuana.

There was a time when, presented with these outrages, Christians would unite, take a stand, and quickly bring decency back into equilibrium with a free society. That time is gone, and that is why we are in *this* time. Did unbelievers advance or did believers retreat?

## Crocodile Tears

Of course, the world we live in today is in much worse condition than these quaint examples indicate. Within the last 10 years, unbelievers have turned to packing courts and voting into office media-created candidates who forcefully insert a pagan agenda into the very laws of our land. They have bribed voters with promises of unearned redistributed wealth while they imported non-citizens to out-vote us. They have installed leaders in place who arrogantly claim the right to determine which laws they will or will not enforce despite their oaths to uphold the entire law of the land. They have even fooled self-professing Christians into joining their ranks.

Despite crocodile tears while championing "tolerance," the attacks by unbelievers against Christians have been relentlessly brutal. G. K. Chesterton, a 20th century English theologian and philosopher, once wrote that touting the "virtue of tolerance is all that remains after a man has lost all his principles." Abandoning all principles except "tolerance," they have employed brute-force bully tactics to route their agenda right around our Constitution. They have stomped on our faith, slithered deep into our families and homes, and wrapped themselves ever tighter around our very own children.

They are lost, and we are to share the good news of Christ's redemption with them. But we must never forget that left unrepentant, unbelievers who attack Christianity are very, very dangerous. We must not engage without the full backing of our Lord and His guidance. We must love them with His love, but not become them or allow ourselves to be overtaken by them. The church is to be a window to God, not a mirror to the world.

The enemies of Christ are well aware that the family is the root foundation of all government. It is the family they are destroying. For without the foundational strength of the family, government no longer has the power to reflect family values as societal norms. It's a free-for-all. And they think that is what they want. If we continue to retreat, they shall complete their mission with zero casualties, all at a very cheap price indeed. In many cases, their own history with us has taught them that a simple "BOO" can do the trick. Watch as they threaten a small and financially tight school district with a lawsuit. Immediately, innocent Christmas pageants and joyous Christmas carols are gone from that school district forever, never to return. And soon (ultimately), we shall whisper them only in our closets, if we dare.

Many Christians are only now just discovering they have spent the last decade in a pan of comfortably warm water that has now come to full boil. If we don't get out of that pan while we still can, it's over. The Christian influence in America will be relegated to outlaw status, leaving our nation ripe for conquest.

As dire as this sounds, take heart. Darkness cannot overtake light. It's impossible. Light a tiny match, and darkness must run for cover. The two cannot exist in the same space. Let me reiterate: darkness can only fill a space vacated by light. It has no power over light. None.

This book trumpets the return of the Christian. *The Stand* is Volume I of a three-volume *Return of the Christian* series. This series constitutes a manifesto call to action in response to the historic times wherein we find ourselves in this morning of the 21$^{st}$ century. Volume II, *On the March*, picks up the call, once we are standing, to march forward, in faith and according to God's will, toward the adversary. Volume III, *Engage!*, culminates the call to action to gain evangelistic ground through the Gospel, promulgated by a unified church of Bible-believing Christians. As God begins to bring about the most dramatic riptide change this world has ever seen, Christians across the globe are sending the signals. They've heard their Lord. They're ready to take a stand.

The singular theme of this manifesto is simply this: *darkness cannot advance unless light retreats.* And so, first, we shall stand…

## Chapter One

# First Things First

Take heart! The power of God is immeasurable, and it's on your side. Your salvation in Christ is a connection to a formidable power, one tiny burst of which created millions of suns and planets. And yet all of it voluntarily bled to death to reconcile man and God! Yes, there is power in that blood and you are by no means insignificant to God. In fact, quite the opposite is true. By comparison, let us now take a quick look at the "power" unbelievers have wielded against the one true God and His children. It may seem formidable when we compare it to ourselves as individuals, but it cannot produce so much as a squeak against the power we have in Christ.

Unbelievers seem to have not only risen to the pinnacle of their agenda, but have continued past that point to suppress nearly every Christian voice in the public square. How did this happen? We will address this question, but rest assured, the *Return of the Christian* outlines a manifesto that asks not "What has happened?" but rather "What shall we do now?"

If you spend time on social media, or if you are involved in your community or in political, civic or church groups, you have to fight the twin temptations of discouragement and anger. There is absolute validity to the concept of "righteous anger," but an angry Christian is quite a different matter and oxymoronic to our faith. As for discouragement, our faith counters this pitfall by the certain truth of God's promises. This book is designed to encourage you to move forward into biblical action, and out of the stasis of intimidation and discouragement. Our goal is to unite all Christians under

God's purpose that both marches before you and stands behind you.

In the first chapter of the Gospel of John, we learn that we who have received Christ were given the right, even the authority, to be called "Children of God" (John 1:12). We are members of God's royal family. Our home is in heaven, not here. But the last passage in Matthew gives us a clear mission to perform while we are here on Earth. So here we are, empowered by God Himself through the Holy Spirit, yet trapped in a flesh-centric body in a broken world. Although we are saved, we are embroiled in a war we didn't start, but one our Savior will certainly finish. If we are honest with each other, we will admit that at one time, we were on the other side. We Christians, in a sense, are turncoats in this struggle.

As for our own individual salvation, that war *is finished*. Jesus Christ snatched us away from a well-earned eternal sentence in darkness. Yet we still battle sin as it relentlessly attempts to invade our bodies, our lives, our precious children, our communities, our country, and indeed, the entire world. Amidst this onslaught, we have been commissioned to go and teach all that Jesus has commanded and baptize those who accept His free gift of eternal life in the name of the Father, the Son, and the Holy Spirit (Matthew 28:19-20). Why then do we still encounter conflict with sin?

Even though we have been saved eternally, temporally (in this time) we are still residing in a broken world with our mission still to accomplish. But unlike the unbeliever, we are at total peace with God, the ultimate victor of this war, the Creator and Chief Executive Officer of the universe and everything in it. That's a very good place to be. We chose wisely. We are in that place, in no way by our own ability, but by His overflowing grace alone. But it gets even better. Our faith is based on His promise that He will return to claim us and put a final end to this onslaught of sin we face each day. It is our faith in His astounding work on the cross, and His unbounded love for us, that carries us through spiritual battle. For greater is He who is in us, than he who is in the world (1 John 4:4).

**Bunker Down Or Stand Our Ground?**

Yet, we say to ourselves more often than not, "The deck is so stacked against us, what in the world can we possibly do down here that is anything resembling effective?" This reasoning tends to run us into a kind of cryogenic preservation. What real contribution can we make in a world that is literally hell-bent? We appear to have lost tremendous ground. When the entire world government turns against God, as it seems to us today, what chance do we have to make any difference at all? Perhaps our best option is just to go underground until the Lord returns? However, if we freeze ourselves into a deep sleep until the day of His return, we will have taken the single talent he gave us to invest and, instead, buried it (Matthew 25:25-30). No, we must fight the good fight and run the race to the finish as that great "cloud of witnesses" cheers us on (Hebrews 12:1-2).

Here in the United States, it seems we vote, vote, vote, without making any difference at all. We are watching as our fellow citizens knowingly and repeatedly elect false leaders who promise their supporters that they are in on the scam and will be protected, while godly people pay the consequences and pick up the tab. They wink at each other in the tenuous belief that they shall both mutually benefit from such deception.

But of course, the inevitable occurs. We watch as even those supporters have the tables turned on them by their co-conspirators, and we see them paying dearly for the irresponsible abrogation of their civic duties. Yet these people, apparently refusing to believe they've allowed themselves to be duped, double down in their defiance of God and even the Constitution of their country.

We are experiencing a very faint shadow of what hell on Earth must be like. The day is coming when not a shred of the Holy Spirit will be present and unbelievers will turn on each other completely. Then, what shall they do in that day? No Christian wants anyone to see that day, yet we know that many who today are exalted and claiming victory will suffer horribly. In that day, no common enemy called "Christian" will remain within their reach. In that day, deception will no longer be utilized or required. With the light gone, no pretense or conspiracy will be necessary. Exactly when that day will come, no one knows but our Father in heaven, but we know it is most certainly coming. These glimpses we see today only compel us to share the Gospel all the more.

We warned them as we preached the Gospel, did we not? Yet they center their lives on sin in the mistaken belief that its inevitable consequences will simply evaporate if only more join in their web of deception. Any believer who attempts to warn about the horrible, unavoidable consequences of sin is immediately "sacrificed" on their "progressive" altar of the "greater good." To them, we are purveyors of doom, when in fact, we bring truth and good news. [*The Greek root word, from which we derive the English word "Gospel," literally translates as "good news."*] Both our message, and we ourselves, are perceived as bad news because we shine a very bright and uncomfortable light into their resident darkness, where all sorts of depravity is propagating in the very shadow of daylight.

They are evangelists of darkness, selling a "new enlightenment" for a "new age." But it's the same ancient attempt to sell rejection of Christ by pulling the wool over the eyes of a potentially ignorant generation. This "new freedom" is nothing more than that old serpent singsong in Eve's ear. Satan has very few tricks. You either love God or you want to be your own god. These snake oil merchants are actually working toward enveloping the world in darkness while deeming it "light." They are going to "enlighten" the world by bringing it under complete darkness, if they can. Since we carry the light of Christ's salvation, we cannot exist in that world, anymore than they can exist in the light. Their only hope is salvation in Christ, freely offered. But it is a limited time offer. In the meantime, our nation remains divided.

## Is Political Power The Answer?

In the United States of America, we must not fall into the temptation of blaming our political leaders for divisiveness and polarization. We pine and lament that our government leaders just can't seem to cooperate or accomplish anything. However, in this country, we, the people, are the government. The government is not a separate entity from the people. If the government of the United States is divided, it is because its people, who elected their representatives, are divided. We cannot now feign disappointment simply because the complement of our government reflects exactly the complement of a republic divided against itself. Politically, one half tends to cancel out the other half. The power then shifts to those leaders who profess to reside politically in between the two halves. The line of division between the two halves is none other than the narrow zone between light and darkness. In a real (albeit accidentally humorous) sense, we tend to elect candidates from the "The Twilight Zone." We've come to believe that this stalemate is the best we can expect. But this compromised equilibrium is unsustainable.

Certainly, one side seems to be winning at the moment. This is only because they are united in their enmity toward Christianity. What strange bedfellows political liberals and progressives are! They do not want government intrusion in the womb, the bedroom, and now the wedding chapel, but apparently crave it everywhere else. They fiercely protect a woman's right to murder her baby in the womb, for no reason other than convenience, but will howl bloody murder against a deer hunt to control the deer population. If unbelievers are going to take up arms against God, they are going to have to be a bit more consistent or they shall dissolve into chaos. Rarely do they admit it, but Christianity is their sworn enemy. Even Muslims and illegal immigrants are granted special rights not visible in the U.S. Constitution, while basic civil liberties are denied to Christians.

We will examine a recent case of such discrimination in the next chapter. Make no mistake about it; this is a war against Jesus and all those who claim Him. We are not commissioned by our Lord to establish a vigilante army; nor are we to take arms against the lost. We have only to obey our Lord, and He shall enable us to stand in victory for His Glory, in His way, and on His clock.

As a first step, we have to be honest with ourselves. I doubt seriously that we Christians have been completely loyal to our Lord when faced with such challenges. Opportunities to stand our Christian ground have been scandalously squandered over the years, usually by the spiritually timid who hide behind the false twin banners of "peace and unity." If we examine our walk with Christ honestly and thoroughly, all of us, myself included, are guilty. We will discuss this in more detail later. For now we shall allow such a provocative statement to stand for consideration because we have a more pressing question ahead of us.

## What Must We Do Now?

We are in a spiritual battle, and that battle is the Lord's; therefore, the most important thing we must do is pray. We must pray together and pray often. It sounds like a cliché, I know; but don't you see? A lack of effective prayer is the root cause of our problems and the primary reason we are trapped down in the rabbit hole. If we view prayer as a cliché response to a first order call to action, we have forgotten the enormous, mushroom-cloud power of prayer.

You might be saying to yourself right now, "Is that all this guy has to offer? Prayer? I thought this book was a manifesto. I can read a thousand books on prayer. When is someone going to come along and show me how to stand and fight? That's what I want to hear!"

We will get there.

You will indeed discover the Christian soldier within you by the time you finish this book. But a soldier who rushes into battle without communication and orders is unarmed, suicidal, and doomed before he starts. Before any soldier picks up a weapon, he must be able to communicate with his superiors. Otherwise how will he know where to go, what weapon to carry, or what target to secure? First, we set up our communications infrastructure, our logistics pipeline. That means establishing consistent and reliable prayer and a unified fellowship. Then, very soon, we will assume our other martial duties, donning our full armor to stand, march, and engage. Don't be a Luke Skywalker, rushing off into battle alone and unarmed. Whatever brought us to this moment, this time we are going to fight God's way, with one or with a million.

**We've Been Here Before**

Our generation is not the first to face this great challenge. Let's look at Gideon, who took up arms against the Midianites in the Old Testament. Israel had done evil in the sight of the Lord, and so He gave His children over to the enemy who ravaged the land repeatedly and drove their victims to the caves. Gideon's divine charter begins in Judges 6:12. Like many of us, Gideon wasn't sure he heard God's direction correctly. Though a mighty warrior, he obviously had some communications problems and trust issues with God. After repeated attempts to secure divine assurance of success, Gideon responded by marshalling a huge, overwhelming army. But God had a different plan. If you have never read the biblical account showing how God brought Gideon's army to victory with a mere 300 men and few weapons, stop now. Read the story of this battle focusing on Judges, chapter 7. It will astound you and set the table for our manifesto.

God's Word is our primary source of information about God, how He works with us, and how we benefit from His grace even as we live out our own generation. As you keep coming back to His Word, you will find that even when the times change, the situations remain essentially the same. For instance, metaphorically speaking, would you consider that many Christians today are "fleeing for the caves?" If you know your Bible and are in God's Word daily, then you realize godly people have often been in this situation. If you read your Old Testament, you know of many accounts of great faith and upheavals of fortune. They can teach us today. It is certainly an over-simplification, but the root cause of downward societal trends seems to be the habitually poor choices of citizens, judges and lawmakers alike. Rather than striving for godliness, they pander to the lowest common denominator, which in turn, drives wrong decisions on both domestic and foreign policy fronts. Rather than responding with prayer and humility, they say, "That's fine, God. We can take it from here; thanks and have a nice day!"

The minute we think things are going our way, we tend to disconnect the power cord. We coast a little further by our previous momentum, but very soon we crawl to a stop. We need to stay continually connected to the power of the Holy Spirit. When we do, we stay on course, which enables us to tap even more of that power. That power, in turn, then multiplies across an ever-growing fellowship of believers. Nothing can stand in the way of such indomitable power. It is within our grasp. It's ours to use for His glory. The best news of all is there is no power bill. It's free!

## Chapter Two

# Politics and Religion: Oil and Water?

The American political landscape is fraught with pitfalls for the biblical Christian. Pure political agendas, by their very nature, contain within their scope elements that are foreign to biblical theology. This is true no matter what end of the political spectrum you reside in at any given moment. So before we get into all of this, we need to set the table with a primer. Despite the old adage that politics and religion don't mix, they are, in fact, inseparable.

It is impossible for man to separate his belief system from his political actions, for one drives the other. During every election the electorate demands a complete understanding of the candidate's belief system and his worldview, as an indication of his projected performance in office. He who demands absolute divorcement from one's belief system in politics contradicts himself the minute he votes in the polling booth.

Our system previously worked because Americans always assumed the candidate, once elected, would in any case conform to the Constitution, in accordance with the oath of office. Yet recently, we have seen that this is no longer a reliable assumption.

First let's define the essential terms. The world defines "religion" as a belief system associated with either a superhuman or a higher power. The term "politics" is generally defined as a system of beliefs associated with the activities and governance of a particular country or principality.

## The Constitution – A Unifying Document

As outlined in the Constitution, the United States government prioritizes by politics while the church prioritizes by religion. Contrary to popular belief, the Constitution does not set these two at odds. There has always been overlap from the beginning. Despite improper interpretations of the Establishment Clause over the years, they are not now (nor have they ever been) mutually exclusive. The Establishment Clause in the first amendment states that government shall not establish any religion as the governing power over the people as had been done at times in European history. The clause does not prohibit or exclude those activities across the two positions, which do not supplant the power of the people to govern themselves under the Constitution. The Founding Fathers recognized that the two, when in proper balance, complemented each other precisely because they are inseparable within the soul of man.

The document that binds our nation actually harmonizes the natural blending of the two belief systems into a democratic form of government, which recognizes the inalienable rights of a free people under God. The Constitution (and the Declaration of Independence) recognizes that man cannot grant or limit these rights because they are inherited naturally from our Creator. In the proper execution of both politics and religion, action is justified as originating from a higher source rather than from any one human being, church, or political party. In politics the higher source is the people and the people are under God.

## Challenges To Liberty

At the time this book was written, Americans were enduring the sixth year of President Obama's administration here in the United States. Of course, one cannot lay the entire blame on a particular leader, party, or even politics in general. But the coincidence is at least clear. Christians were stunned over those six years at how quickly the moral and political landscape has changed. Certainly the Obama administration contributed heavily to that changed landscape. During that time, something new and singularly attributable to the Obama administration had intruded from the political landscape into our deepest personal affairs.

History will record that the Obama administration initiated an entirely new angle of attack on the personal liberty of Christians and unbelievers alike. It crossed heretofore-unreachable boundaries by the deliberate and active insertion of the executive branch, and particularly the Department of Justice, into the public square. Never before have we seen such wanton and dominant intrusion into our most sacred thoughts, rights, and beliefs. The Department of Justice, as directed by the president, laid all other priorities aside to support states that adopted a "progressive" agenda. Conversely, it forcefully asserted itself deep into state's rights, intervening and circumventing those state governments that insisted on preserving those rights the Constitution reserved solely for them.

This unprecedented executive branch intrusion even strives to determine who is allowed to vote for federal office in each state and how those voters are verified, if at all. The Voter Protection Act is on the books, but every time a state passes legislation to identify a bona fide voter, the Department of Justice stomps in, with federal taxpayer money, to shut it down cold. Any American would have to ask why the federal government exerts such a herculean effort against states that are simply trying to maintain an elementary level of election integrity. Simultaneously, laws firmly in place to protect our own borders go unenforced by the very same executive branch, sworn to uphold the entire law of the land.

President Obama's executive branch affects every person in the country regarding his right to choose his own health care as it frequently "changes" signed Affordable Care Act legislation. That landmark legislation itself was forced into the public square, right down to requiring Christians to pay for abortion. Never receiving one vote from the opposition party, it consumes one-sixth to one-fifth of the entire economy. Then-Senate Majority leader Reid changed the rules of the senate, literally at the last minute to avoid a filibuster, so that only 51 votes were needed in the Senate to pass the bill. It was passed in the dead of the night and, as Americans discovered later, not one congressman or senator who voted for it ever read it in its entirety or had any real understanding of what was in it. Sadly, we have since learned that the president himself, by executing purposefully planned deception upon the American people, is the primary reason it passed at all.

President Obama's executive branch even asserts unfounded authority to determine what property you actually have a right to own, whether the subject is "gun control" or eminent domain. Not content with these outrageous intrusions, the executive branch has launched a full-scale intrusion deep into every method of private communication by every human being in the country, and arguably, the entire world. The Obama administration has stretched, by executive fiat, the original limitations of the Patriot Act far beyond the borders established by the original legislation.

The last executive action outrage before this book went to press was the president's move to disregard existing law on immigration rather than negotiating with the people's representatives whose sole duty it is to legislate law. The president may be tired of waiting for legislation, but Congress, the people's representatives, are allowed their vote and their say in the constitutional process. The president's eraser is more fearsome than his pen. With the stroke of an imperial eraser, the house of the people is heard no more.

In countless executive branch scandals, wholesale corruption involving just about every cabinet level position has been employed to silence and sabotage legitimate political opponents.

Though unbelievers collectively winked at each other to bring to bear this preposterous abuse of power, they obviously never dreamt it would come back to haunt them. They are now subject to the same abuses they conspired to enact on believers, for a power-drunk government is unable to distinguish friend from foe in its bleary-eyed binge. Their anticipated protection, if it ever existed, is gone forever.

After the 2014 midterm election, they are now reshuffling their belief systems, yet again, to determine their next move. If this massive encroachment on the personal freedom of every American is not reversed, what will prevent the next president of a different party from continuing to abuse the Constitution? When the Constitution is abandoned, every American is a victim. When Christ is abandoned every human being suffers.

As outrageous as these political attacks are on our freedom as Americans and our freedom to exercise our faith, we must not be completely and fully drawn in politically to the exclusion of the spiritual.

## Christianity Vs. Religion And Why It Matters

Before we go any further, I would parenthetically point out that Christianity is not understood by biblical Christians to be a religion; rather, it is a personal relationship with the one true living God. In other words, Christianity is not simply a "belief system" based on a "faith process" – the modern definition of religion.

When many of us were younger and had not yet accepted Christ as our Savior, our parents represented the sum total authority in our lives. There were rules and rituals (some of these we called "chores"), which provided a path for our growth. This personal and dependant relationship cannot be described with any degree of accuracy by using such a dubious moniker as religion. "Hello, Principal Roberts, I would like you to meet my belief system, Joyce and John Feet." Obviously, our parents were not a system. They were real people who resided with us. We talked and consulted with them. We took their direction when we obeyed. We received their discipline when we weren't so good. We constantly pleaded our case to them, and relied completely upon them for our very sustenance. This was a loving, nurturing, and personal relationship; and yes, it included a certain authoritative element. This personal relationship with our parents mimics the essence of a Christian's relationship with Jesus Christ. No wonder the family structure is under attack!

In contrast, the world can only define religion as a belief system outside of the knowledge of a personal relationship with Christ.

Because unbelievers have rejected Christ, they can only describe Christianity as though it were designed to provide comfort, assurance, and guidance. The world defines this as religion. But we reject this worldly terminology as a belief system because it is associated with a papier-mâché god that does not exist.

Even some of our greatest Christian theologians, dating back to the early church fathers, have used the term *religion* to describe our belief system in their work. But their use of the term was not in the modern vernacular. Not surprisingly then, this was the context within which our Founding Fathers used the term in our founding documents.

**Christianity And The Constitution – Putting It All Together**

The Establishment Clause in the first amendment of the Constitution states:

*"Congress shall make no law respecting an establishment of religion, or prohibiting the free exercise thereof."*

Even though we have noted that the term religion does not accurately apply to Christianity, that assertion does not place Christianity outside the constraints of the Establishment Clause. The clause rightly addresses the sordid history of placing a religion in power *over* the government of the people. Our Founding Fathers knew their history and were well aware of the disastrous results that have always ensued under such a system.

We have put forth the notion that politics and religion are actually inseparable, tempered in this country by our Constitution. Nowhere in the Constitution does the term "separation of church and state" exist.

*[In fact, judicial tinkering with the Establishment Clause, including introducing*

*terms like "wall of separation," did not begin until 1947 (Everson v Board of Education). Even then, the court upheld that the state could and should pay for bussing to and from parochial schools.]*

Note the other half of the clause: "or prohibiting the free exercise thereof." The Establishment Clause is balanced at both ends. Its intent is that neither end should hold power over the other. By this precise wording of the Establishment Clause, our Founding Fathers recognized that government and religion naturally coexist alongside one another. Only in recent history have attempts been made by the Supreme Court to upset that balance.

And finally, we have noted the recent unprecedented government intrusion into the public square. If we are indeed to discover the true relationship between politics and religion, we would keep these points in mind, developing them as the basis for defining and understanding how they influence each other.

## Two Battlefields And Where They Meet

In future volumes, we will delve deeper into how the twin universes of politics and religion interweave, but for this volume, we are primarily concerned with reversing our collective lethargy and bracing for a stand, so that no more ground shall be surrendered.

In every battle, each side eventually settles on a clear strategic path and a decided battlefield. The aggressor almost always chooses the battlefield. Unbelievers in the United States, as the aggressors, have clearly chosen a *political* battlefield. This strategy, for the short term, is certainly working for them; but the fissures are beginning to show. We must remember that their strategy is fraught with its own perils. It does not rely on a single unchanging foundation such as God's Word. Unbelievers cannot even stand on the Constitution as their foundation, since they must pervert it to achieve their own ends. The political landscape ever changes. Those who choose to be adversaries of our Lord, by embracing politics as their religion, tenuously grasp a very slippery bar of soap. This is because employing politics in the United States, as a tool to advance one's particular belief system to the detriment of all others, requires a constant effort to extirpate the Constitution from the process. All political activity in this country is conducted under that single foundational document. A true patriot does not argue for adoption of his own feelings and opinions, nor even his own beliefs isolated from the Constitution. He argues adherence to the Constitution or the consensual amendment thereof.

To the extent a political group's belief system aligns with the Constitution, political efficiency results. However, if that belief system does not align with the Constitution, considerable effort, circumlocution and continuous deception must be expended. It requires a severe energy drain and consistent discipline to maintain an improvised manifesto. Without the solid foundation of the Constitution, such a manifesto changes as frequently as any one member of the fragile alliance can change his mind.

That is why the Christian's battlefield is spiritual, and not political. If constantly changing political worldviews swayed the Christian, it would force him to constantly realign his relationship with Christ, as his own changing worldview would constantly clash with God's Word. This would be impossible to reconcile because God's Word is unchanging. Mankind's advancement and enlightenment (I am referring to these terms facetiously) have no bearing on God's settled Word. Therefore, the Christian is always in line with God's Word and is always at peace with what "ought to be." The unbeliever is constantly reforming and reshaping his chosen political battlefield, while the Christian stands on solid, unchanging, and unshakable spiritual ground.

The Christian concentrates on increasing and growing Christ-likeness in an overall forward trend, despite any personal and temporary setbacks in his relationship with God. We know what we ought to do, and this is unchanging. We are daily driven to our Lord for guidance, encouragement, and correction in dealing with the obstacles that temporarily block our way. Unlike the unbeliever, we never, ever need ask, "What is the basis of my faith today, as opposed to yesterday?" This represents a superior advantage over any worldly adversary.

In this manner then, Christians should always be solidly united in their ideology, their foundation unthreatened by the changing world around them. If your church is changing its operating mode, you need to be sure it is adapting only its method of communicating the Gospel to meet the world where it is, rather than changing the Gospel itself. Many churches and politicians alike, pleading the threat of isolation, have ditched their biblical foundation and are now, ironically, isolated.

Note that unbelievers do believe in *something*. But that something keeps changing. How many times have we heard that the views of politicians, organizations, and even churches have "evolved?" It is an indisputable fact that unbelievers, driven by their belief of the day, inject that belief forcefully, relentlessly, and sometimes brutally into their political agenda. In fact, it is solely their belief of the day that drives their politics. They disingenuously do not refer to their beliefs as their religion, but the convictions of their beliefs reflect, to the letter, the definition of religion. That religion is very quickly becoming the Law of the Land.

We must remind the world that Christians in America have never pursued a similar political movement against unbelievers. A direct corollary would be for Christians to inject their belief system into the law in violation of the

Constitution. This is exactly what unbelievers do. If Christians were to attempt the same action, the result would be to replace our representative republic with a theocracy. Unbelievers accuse us of this constantly, but our legislative and political actions merely seek to move our country back to the neutral ground of our representative republic and realign it with the Constitution, *never to a theocracy*. It seems we are always in repair mode, having never dreamt we would have to pass legislation whose core is already codified in the Constitution. We have never done to them what they are doing to us. Ever. We are incapable, by our very faith itself, of bringing about such a coup.

## One Skirmish And Its Implications

One recent example out of thousands says it all. In early 2014, you may have heard about a Christian-owned bakery that politely and apologetically refused to bake a cake for a same-sex wedding. The couple could have just chosen another business to patronize (they did) and left it at that (they didn't). They could have exercised their propagandist message of "coexist," respecting someone else's faith without any compromise to their own. But no, they marshaled political forces to sue and attempt to put this particular bakery out of business. Not lost on any Christian is the imminent intimidation of any and all Christians who might do likewise. That state conducted an investigation and concluded the bakery violated the couple's basic civil rights and unlawfully discriminated against them.

Without even considering the other side of the Establishment Clause regarding the free exercise of religion, the state easily slammed the gavel down in favor of the plaintiff. Why? Their allies had previously laid the groundwork by quietly passing state legislation that added onto existing anti-discrimination law what was not there before–homosexuality as a civil right on par with an historical struggle against racial inequality. However, the Bible tells us unequivocally that homosexuality is a behavior, not an intrinsic attribute.

The state ruled the bakery did not have the right to refuse service based on sexual orientation as passed in new legislation. By this law, no Christian who goes into business can abide in his faith while faithfully serving his country and his customers. This has never before been the case in the United States of America. It is now. At the time this book went to press, the bakery was under court order to violate its faith and lend its artistry and labor in support of any and all same-sex weddings solicited by any customer. Additionally, it is under court order to report every three months on its conformance to this order. Thus a Christian-owned industry is under order by the government to report to the government all same-sex weddings supported or denied during that period. What would you do in such a situation? I ask because it is coming your way even now.

Note that unbelievers initiated the battle. All was in equilibrium until the couple disturbed it and purposely placed the bakery into an unnecessary dilemma. Even those who give government the benefit of the doubt can safely assume the recently passed laws were not designed to protect the safety and security of the citizenry, but to facilitate actual confrontation. It was state law that resulted in the bakery's loss of suit and concurrent punishment. This is an excellent example of unbelievers utilizing their faith to initiate battle on their chosen battlefield.

The bakery was passive, the couple active. The plaintiffs had zero regard for the honest beliefs of the bakery's owners, who were simply living by their own faith, forcing it on no one. That Christian faith, established and completed over 2000 years ago, has not changed one iota. This instance is not "coexistence" as one popular multi-icon bumper sticker promises. It is a wholesale attack with the intent to destroy the livelihood and wipe from the public square those who do not share the same belief.

What do Christians do in such a situation? We are called to share the light of truth in all circumstances. In this case, the official ruling states that a non-religious enterprise cannot discriminate in any manner against any religion, race, color, creed, or sexual orientation. That enterprise must sell its goods to anyone regardless of these factors, according to state law. Our response as Christians is to first apply God's Word. Jesus and His disciples used logic in their defense many times. This logic is based on The One who has proven Himself to be the way, *the truth,* and the life (John 14:6).

In an unbelieving world we can still apply truth and logic to test the validity of such a law. That unbelievers reject Christ is evidence they do not base decisions entirely on logic. Yet they claim logic and reason as their basis to declare Christianity illogical. This has led the entire world, from man's expulsion from the Garden of Eden to the present, into an awful mess from which only Christ can rescue us. Yet those who lay the traps often step into them. We must remember that the tides of tyranny often reverse with whiplash alacrity. "What's good for the goose is good for the gander," reflects our experience that some things can come back to haunt us.

In light of this truth, let's look more closely at the potential ramifications of the bakery case. Many people have since commented in various forums on the illogical conclusions reached by the state. A few examples, taken in the aggregate, reflect our collective head scratching. For instance, if a KKK member walked into an African-American-owned bakery and ordered a cake with a decorative burning cross (however distasteful this would be), the bakery must provide that service, according to current law. On the other side of the looking glass, many states protect the open carry of firearms but allow stores and restaurants to expel those who exercise this constitutional right. Under the law we have discussed, it isn't a stretch to demand now that all shops require acceptance and service to anyone who carries a gun into their place of business.

This is but a sample of the confusion resulting from subsequent rulings based on such legislation. As happens more often than not in the United States, each new law tends to complicate a whole host of existing laws. But our purpose is not to be diverted and then bogged down into the political mire of confusion the adversary has chosen as its battleground.

## A Christian Response

The examples above only demonstrate the tangled web we enter when Christians reactively respond in battle on the same ground as their adversaries. Their ever-changing ground, their constantly morphing ideology, is quite often most untenable ground indeed. It is certainly never fully compatible with our faith. Should we be politically active? Yes, of course. But we should render unto Caesar that which belongs to Caesar and render unto God that which belongs to God. In politics, Christians in America should stand on the Constitution, their involvement led by God. In spiritual issues, we shall be led by the power of the Holy Spirit.

We are fortunate that our Constitution employs strong elements of Christianity as its basis. So much so, that under our Constitution, our political efforts often align closely with our relationship with Christ. After all, that was the whole point upon which the Founding Fathers risked their lives, their fortunes, and their sacred honor. It has served all American citizens well.

But we must never forget that the battle is spiritual and belongs to the Lord. It must be fought with spiritual weapons. We have been suffering under the mistaken impression that the battle must be primarily fought in the political realm. Since politics and religion are inseparable, this mistake is quite understandable. But God did not send political operatives into the world. He sent his only Son, and subsequently, all who believe in Him to take up His cross (His example).

Although accused as such by many religious leaders of his day, Jesus was not a political operative when He walked this Earth. He has since risen and ascended to His throne. He has fulfilled His prophesied role as the meek, suffering Savior. By His work on the cross and His anointing by the Father, He is the King of Kings and will come to claim His Kingdom. You'd better believe he has some "political" action to take in that coming day when all kings and all nations will bow before Him. At the risk of sounding repetitive, remember that the battle is His and He is on His throne, regardless of whatever we may be experiencing here and now.

We must not get suckered into deploying all our forces onto the political battlefield in a spiritual war. To continue is to ignore our most powerful advantage. Wise spiritual warriors target the spirit. All this time, the adversary has been fighting the war on the wrong battlefield – *politi*cs; and we fecklessly followed them there.

What is required is an outflanking maneuver. Unbelievers place all of their resources, fortune, and personnel into the political swamp and muck of their chosen battlefield. That very ground undermines them, while often trapping Christians in the mire. While we have a place in the political dialogue, Christians should concentrate on the spirit and soul of the unbeliever. It is his soft-underbelly, as it were. The unbeliever has not, and cannot, build up a viable spiritual defense when he has starved the spirit of any real fortification. The worst we face is a heart fortified only by a shifting and unstable political battleground. God's love can penetrate the hardest heart that, at any point, begins to question its own shaky ground. The unbeliever is not yet permanently the property of Satan. That is where we come in.

How have unbelievers been able to take over this country on their chosen battlefield, when God himself could negate their actions with a single thought? What actions have you and I, Christian, implemented during this takeover? I don't think we can blame God.

We have to ask ourselves then, what is holding us back from conducting a concentrated spiritual *offensive* against the darkness that threatens to envelop us? There can only be one answer: Fear.

# Chapter Three

# What Are We Afraid Of?

*[Have your sword (your Bible) handy from here on in. We will be referring to it often rather than reprinting large portions of scripture here. When I place a scriptural reference in the text, my intention is for you to stop and read the full biblical reference in your Bible before picking up again in our text. In this way, you can study the reference from your own favorite translations rather than relying on the author's choice. Just make sure you are working from a universally accepted translation. I advise using at least two different translations from your library in order to capture the full context of the scripture passage. You don't have to do this of course, but if you*

*can, you are in for a rich experience! You do want to get your money's worth, don't you?]*

Today's believers, facing real battles, can learn to boldly "fight like men." There is a difference between outright fear and having the wisdom to know when, where, and how to engage. For far too long, the Christian has been driven by the unbeliever's schedule. The cycle is familiar. A group of unbelievers join to push the envelope, usually by restricting freedom once acceptable in the public square or by introducing behavior that was never before acceptable. Next, they sit back and wait for the howling to start. Finally, they claim persecution and victimization when Christians respond. I think we now know this routine by heart.

**Our Response: Two Paths**

There are two responses we should consider: the long-term path and the more immediate short-term path. The long-term path, and the ultimate thrust of the *Return of the Christian* series, is to proactively share the Gospel. Notice that when we *share*, we are incapable of forcing our belief on others. We shall share the pure Gospel as it convicts, encourages, and changes hearts and minds to a point where Christians are no longer politically outnumbered. This is a natural progression when the truth is not suppressed. In this way, the nation will eventually vote and politically operate itself as originally intended under the Constitution. *We do not preach politics.* Man's politics naturally follows his worldview; witness the authorship of the Constitution by godly men over two hundred years ago. If we consistently teach the Gospel, we will return to a Bible-believing nation. The politics of our representative republic under the Constitution will then take care of itself. History shows this to be absolutely true. Such is the power of the Gospel. But if Christians allow themselves to be bullied into silence, the nation is bereft of the benefit of the Gospel.

Again, we are not initiating a revolutionary call to install a theocracy. We are working to restore the original underpinning of our constitutional government here in the United States, where all competing worldviews enjoy the same rights of protection. Secondarily, we are working to ensure that Christian principles are not forcibly ripped from the public square. We have a right to stand and protect our principles from those who seek not to coexist, but to wipe out Christianity entirely. If Christianity is left unfettered to stand side-by-side with competing values, the choice is always clear. Many groups of unbelievers in the United States are very much aware of this and strive relentlessly to silence any views but their own. Christians have a right to coexist with other competing worldviews, and we shall stand to the death, if necessary, on that right.

But the long-term solution depends on the short-term solution, which is to stand fast and not give ground. In triage language, this is known as "stopping the bleeding." Both response paths require the courage of our faith and convictions. In order to map them out, we must first examine the actions and history that led us to where we are today. Armed with that information, we can make corrections, institute improvements, and perfect our stand. Only then can we march forward and engage to take back lost ground.

From scenarios like the bakery example in chapter two, in which the unbeliever has initiated what amounts to an attack on Christianity, history records a typical Christian response: a few stouthearted Christians band together to make what they already know is an Alamo-type last stand. They'll do it because they're real spiritual warriors. But most everyone else has gone home and chalked up another victory for Satan. If you chase them down, you'll hear the most pious and cowardly advice ever to tickle your ears: "Well, dear, you know, that's who they are…it's so sad they're lost"; or "It's a little thing really, not a hill to die on"; and the worst, "We are not here to cause animosity, disunity, or initiate controversy. We shall pray for them." If you have ever tried to lead a viable and spiritual defense against a typical attack by unbelievers, these arguments will sound familiar to you. In response, we must remember what Jesus declared when He sent out the twelve disciples.

Our Lord specifically tells us in the Gospel of Matthew that He is sending us out as sheep among wolves, but that we should not fear them. He goes on to describe the divisiveness that will occur as we share the truth (Matthew 10:5-42). This wondrous discourse prepares us for the rocky road that lies before us. It also demonstrates that the Gospel is as much confrontation as it is reconciliation. The clash results only when some not only refuse His offer of eternal life, but also actively conspire against it. You don't get out of this world without choosing sides, as it were. Sadly, many Christians seem to fold up the lawn chair and go home, rather than going forth as Jesus commands. Read this discourse from your Bible now before moving on.

### Here's An Idea: What Does God Say?

I'm not maligning Christians who shirk their biblical duty now and then; I understand they're scared, but they are mistaken about a great many issues. For one thing, they haven't read and prayed over the discourse you just studied in Matthew 10. The need to study the Bible and apply it to our daily lives is essential to the spiritual warrior. The lack of adequate understanding of basic biblical concepts becomes quite apparent when we observe its negative impact. For instance, sometimes as individuals, we correctly absorb the courage of truth the Bible gives us, but then scratch our heads when it doesn't translate well across members of our own churches. This is especially true when a crisis pops up in our church.

I have seen my fair share of church crises. A church crisis is often defined incorrectly as an internal disagreement between Bible-led believers. In fact, I believe a forensic autopsy of every church crisis will show that non-biblical concepts, external to Christianity, were allowed to enter the body of the church unmolested prior to the crisis. Like a disease, these elements grow and fester until they reach a crisis point.

In a typical church crisis, the mistake many people make is to first consider the consequences and probable outcomes of the choices they see before them. Then they work backward to determine which course, if any, will achieve the safest and most satisfactory result. This method sounds reasonable, but this is not biblical. It has a familiar ring to it because it is based on a worldly utilitarian ethic, where the projected outcome justifies the initial course of action, and vice versa. In other words, the course of action is only arrived at once all the possible consequences are considered. Such a process is always fatal to a church. The first question must always be, "What does God say?"

I'm not saying that we should not consider the potential outcomes of our proposed actions. Of course we should. But we should consider the *biblical* consequences over the *worldly*. The church is here to influence the world, not to be influenced by it. This pivotal point of view, our Christian worldview, is critical to Christian decision-making. It is at this decision point, more than any other, where we are likely to fail. We are *in* the world, but not *of* the world.

## Make Up Your Mind Now

Many biblical examples demonstrate the need to firmly make up our minds about how we shall respond to crisis based on scriptural study and consistent prayer. This predetermines our actions long before we are hit with these false worldly dilemmas. Under a utilitarian ethic, Joshua never marches around Jericho; Gideon never whittles his army down to a puny few, obtaining divine victory; and Paul doesn't end up in Rome preaching and teaching deep within the very Roman government out to oppress the embryonic church. I could go on, but I think you get the point. None of these individuals initially set out, by their own determination, to take the exact action God ultimately had planned for them. Likewise, you never know where the Holy Spirit will ultimately take you, and that is a most wondrous thing! Decide first to follow Christ above all. Then the specific response, which may not always be immediately known to us, has already been made and the path firmly set.

Jesus did not follow a utilitarian ethic when He faced His most tortuous choice in the Garden of Gethsemane. The decision to go to the cross had already been made, eons earlier. As Christians, we must already have decided how we are going to respond, long before the response is needed. Then we must always open our hearts to the Holy Spirit to guide us step-by-step. Never forget that our communion with God is ongoing and continuous. We must remain "tuned in" to what God wants for us at all times. This is a two-way dialogue with the Creator of the universe, and not a negotiation exercise. As we openly and intimately discuss our daily challenges with our Lord, our path (from our perspective) may seem to change. But we must remember that it was set from the beginning. As we remain sensitive to the Holy Spirit, communicating our desires and surrendering our will to Him, our path is more sharply revealed.

Even Jesus, one last time, anxiously sought the Father's last word, asking for the cup of crucifixion to be passed but nonetheless that God's will be done (Matthew 26:39). Note the importance of obedience in this exercise, where God is both first and last in the process. We cannot base our decisions on a worldly utilitarian ethic, because our decision base is spiritual. If we did, our faith would be forever thrown into needless turmoil. That turmoil is exactly what the unbeliever experiences every day, although he rarely admits it. Unbelievers require our compassion as we realize what they put themselves through, needlessly, every day. Beware the Christian who attempts to stand on a line between Christ and the world, for "reasonable" compromise is fatal to the salvation of the world and negates Christ's work on the cross.

## Obey God And Leave All The Consequences To Him

In the ultimate example, Jesus told us that the way (to God) is narrow and few find it (Matthew 7:14). In fact, going to the cross actually saves relatively few, if we could compare the numerical total of believers against the sum total of the population of unbelievers throughout history. So why did our Lord voluntarily give up His divinity, all of His power, and submit to the torture and humiliation of the cross for a minority? Humanly speaking, a utilitarian decision by Jesus would have determined that the numbers do not justify the most costly sacrifice in all of history. The end does not justify the means, a clear utilitarian prerequisite. Such a decision would have left all of us doomed to eternal destruction. Along with you, I'm so glad Jesus first asked, "What does the Father say?"

Dr. Charles Stanley, senior pastor of First Baptist Church Atlanta and founder of In Touch Ministries, is well known for sharing probably the most instructive advice ever given to mankind by a single human being: "Obey God, and leave all the consequences to Him." Amen, Dr. Stanley! Why do we tend to first consider the consequences? Because we fear them more than we fear God, and that leads to disobedience.

If you ever find yourself allowing fear to influence a particular choice facing you, I'll guarantee you the "Check Bible" light is solidly lit on your dashboard. Your biblical sensor is not working properly. Address that problem first before making any decision.

## A Healthy Fear Of The Lord

A certain amount of well-placed fear is a healthy commodity. The very essence of fear is a sense that we are in danger of some degree of harm. However, we must access godly wisdom to determine if a particular fear is healthy or not. We know that fear of the Lord is the beginning of all wisdom (Proverbs 1:7); but what does *fear* mean in this context?

Whole books by respected scholars down through the centuries have been written on this subject. We take our guidance from the Bible itself and from those who have, throughout history, devoted their entire lives to theological study. They have proven themselves accepted scholars in their field and in line with scripture. It is beyond the scope of this book to deeply delve into the biblical concept of *fear of the Lord* sufficiently and fully. So put a stake in the ground, as my old professor was fond of saying, and come back to a well developed word study when time permits. However, I offer the following biblical advice to get you started on your own study.

The Hebrew word for fear, and its derivatives, in Proverbs 1:7 is used extensively throughout the Old Testament. In this particular passage, fear is a word designated in Strong's Concordance as 3374 and pronounced "yir'ah." This should be good enough to get you started.

I'm kidding of course. We need a bit more than that. I'm actually trying to use humor to bring up a valid point. Every Christian is responsible to verify against scripture what he or she believes is being taught. Do not trust me (or anyone) solely on the basis of my own word;

verify what I assert through your own responsible biblical study. God's Word is the only basis for any Christian action. If we are going to stand together, we need to be thoroughly convinced by our own individual prayerful study. We stand together on the foundation of God's Word alone, not upon any individual or group.

The word chosen to express fear in Proverbs 1:7 connotes a sense of awe, and even trembling. A healthy dose of respect and reverence is indicated by the context and helps us translate the verse correctly. Yet it would be incorrect to say that the word does not also carry with it some of the traditional sense of fear. So for our unscholarly study, we are very close to a viable translation if we say that the use of the word *fear* here wraps our traditional understanding of the word in a very firm envelope of reverence, respect, and awe.

The core of traditional *fear of the Lord* is anchored in consequences that would occur if we, in the very presence of God, choose to defy

Him. In other words, the real fear is to reject any understanding of the God of the universe and His role in our lives. We reject the wisdom and knowledge of God at our true peril.

The author of Proverbs, traditionally understood to be Solomon in most instances, is telling his son (and all of us by the power of the Holy Spirit) that respect, reverence, and the surrender of our will to God represent the actual beginning of our journey toward godly knowledge, wisdom, and understanding. The antithesis is that we can never hope to begin that journey if we reject God outright. In fact, the antithetical character in this verse is pointed out to be "a fool."

But even that simple explanation of fear does not do this verse justice. Awe and reverence of God usher the lost into acceptance of Christ, and that's when things really start to get interesting. When we accept Christ, He sends the Holy Spirit to dwell in us for the rest of our lives. This powerful connection, God within us, leads to a life-long study of His Word and a life-long personal relationship with the one true God. What an awesome and humbling privilege this is! But it all begins with a continuing desire to seek Him and His wisdom.

## So What Are We Afraid Of?

The only thing the Christian should fear is any hint of separation from God for any amount of time. He should not fear the uninformed criticism of an unbeliever who, by definition, is deceived and seeks earthly rationalization for his actions. The first thing an unbeliever will do is point out any perceived sin he thinks you or any Christian might have committed. He then falsely equates that sin to his own *life of sin* and either brings you artificially across that great divide to the place he resides, or he negates any need to be concerned with sin at all. The epitaph "hypocrite" usually accompanies his pronounced condemnation of the Christian.

What he doesn't understand is the difference between one who rejects God by centering his life on sin (for there is no middle ground between God and sin) and one who accepts God but succumbs to momentary temptation.

When an unbeliever sins, he chooses from an endless menu of worldly explanations to justify his sin as "righteousness." When a Christian sins, he is absolutely in agony and misery until he reconciles with God. This is because sin separates man from God. We have all been there and fear that place the most. In this context, we can make the argument that *fear of the Lord is actually fear of being separated from Him*. On the other hand, the unbeliever feels no misery at all because he is already, by exercising his own free will, separated from God.

## The Outflanking Maneuver

One grave error many Christians commit is to buy the lie that we are worse than the unbeliever because he, at least, makes no pretentions about the *sin* in his life. Christians, the argument goes, are not perfect and therefore contradict themselves daily. They are not to be believed or trusted. They are hypocrites. Faced with this illogical but very effective counterattack, many Christians retreat because they are unprepared biblically to defend their faith (2 Timothy 4:2).

We must not allow unbiblical arguments to characterize Christianity. True, we are not yet perfected because we are still being sanctified. The difference between Christians and unbelievers is that we have surrendered our wills to God, and when we go astray, we seek and accept His promised correction. Rather than downplaying our temporary waywardness, we should instead emphasize, even declare as badges of God's salvation, the very fact that when we sin we run back to Christ. This shamelessly proves to the world our daily need to surrender ourselves to His will and His unbounded love.

If the Christian truly understood the moment-by-moment need to seek and depend on Christ, he would trumpet it from the rooftops. He makes no claim of superiority over the unbeliever. Instead he puts on display, for all to see, both his human fallibility and the unbounded grace of God that saves him. Salvation through Christ truly is the only difference between Christian and unbeliever.

The unbeliever has no such measuring stick, no plumb line to guide him. We see this every day as unbelievers literally celebrate their "no boundaries" mantra. To which we ought to respond, "If something was wrong yesterday but not wrong today, what changed?" When we pose this question, we are really asking, "What, if anything, is wrong anymore and who decides?" Indeed, who but God is qualified to decide?

This is the beginning of the outflanking maneuver we touched on earlier. We must continually probe the belief system of the unbeliever and actively solicit his defense. You might have noticed that it is always the Christian who must defend his stance. Rarely do Christians ever turn the tables to demand a legitimate defense of the unbeliever's basis for his belief. When we do, there can be no satisfactory response because his arguments are self-contradictory. Therefore, we must understand and then repudiate our self-destructive fears in both the spiritual battlefield and the public square.

We have touched very lightly on the self-destructive fears we all face when we take our Christian stand. We understand that we ultimately fear only God, not man. Scripture tells us that unbelievers do not fear God (Romans 3:18). This lack of healthy fear causes them to act rashly, for they think themselves wise, only to be revealed as foolish (Proverbs 1:7; Romans 1:22; Psalm 19).

The unbeliever pushes us back against the wall and demands from us both perfection and absolute proof of God, usually from a disingenuous perspective. We have God's Word, sixty-six books directly inspired by God. All scripture is "God- breathed" (2 Timothy 3:16). Though these books are separated sometimes by centuries, they are totally consistent with each other. They have survived the intense scrutiny of the critics of their day, and of those throughout time. Most importantly, we have Jesus, who demonstrated from His works and His resurrection that He is who He says He is. If He is not, where is the evidence? Finally, we have the Holy Sprit, sent by God, dwelling within us to guide us every moment. We are well-protected and well-armed, but only if we have read and understand the manual on how to use what God has given us. We need to continuously grow in the Word.

The unbeliever will demand evidence of our faith by first demanding we exclude the Bible from discussion. He seems to say, "Show me the evidence of your convictions, outside of all the evidence of your convictions." Sometimes we fall for such a ludicrous premise. Instead, we should be challenging the unbeliever to offer evidence of equal weight against the Bible he is attacking. If we are going to throw out the Bible, we can only do so if new evidence arises to counter and displace its evidentiary claims. This is how every court in the land employs the rules of evidence; and this is what we mean by outflanking and bringing the battle to the spiritual battleground, where it belongs.

As we begin to face and examine the fear that paralyzes us into inaction and retreat, we must grasp these principles. After all, we belong to Christ. We do not belong to our mortgaged house, our job, and our big screen televisions.

Our bodies, though corrupted flesh, are not our own; rather they are temples of the Holy Spirit (1 Corinthians 6:19). Even if we fear loss of possessions or physical pain, we must remember that all belongs to God. Our possessions and our very bodies are temporary, and they all provide service to our ultimate goal: to live for Christ. Our bodies will die, but we are eternal beings. This is true for both Christians and unbelievers who will all be resurrected with new physical bodies. In our new bodies we will either be with God or separated from Him for all eternity.

**You're On The Air...Live!**

There is no dress rehearsal. We are live, on stage now, where it counts. What we do and how we respond to the challenge of the unbeliever today has eternal consequences. Yes, we have a body that experiences both joy and pain. We have temporary comfort and security in material things for ourselves and for our families. We are blessed in many ways. But what manner of profit do we gain if we place these things above our very soul (Matthew 16:26; Mark 8:36; Luke 9:25-26)? Nothing. For if we forfeit it all, it is then all for naught. Everything we physically are and everything we physically own or hope to own is all very sadly (or happily) temporary. If we succumb to fear and do not stand, take up our cross, and follow Christ, we bankrupt ourselves.

No, we must stand. There is nothing they can do to us, unless God allows it; and if God allows it, then it is His will for His glory. For God has never and cannot ever break any of His promises. Blessed are we!

When the Christian puts on the whole armor of God (Ephesians 6:11-20), he arms himself with God's Word, and takes his stand on that Word against those who would attempt to tear it to shreds. For we know that they attack us only to attack Christ (Matthew 5:11). Please take a moment to study the last three biblical references very carefully. If we keep them foremost in our hearts, we shall fear nothing on this earth. Here they are again for your study:

1. Matthew 16:26; Mark 8:36; Luke 9:25-26
2. Ephesians 6:11-20
3. Matthew 5:11

Remember, we are not wrestling with flesh and blood, but against spiritual rulers of the darkness of this age. We do not stand alone. We must *stand* and, having done our all, *we shall remain standing to the end.* On that day every believer and unbeliever shall certainly bow to Christ the King (Romans 14:11). This is a biblical promise upon which we can stand for the rest of our eternal lives.

## Chapter 4

# From Whence We Came

This chapter will be painful to many. In fact, this is going to be the hardest chapter in the book to read because it strikes us so personally. If we are going to relentlessly charge forward with our sword of truth, the Bible, we must first face the truth about ourselves. But when we come out of it on the other side, we will never again have to deal with any self-doubt. Trust me, it is so worth it. Together, let's face those doubts now and allow our Lord to put them to death forever.

Now that we understand the source of our fear, we can fully obey God and leave whatever consequences we might potentially suffer to Him. However, before we overconfidently prepare to smack down the adversary, we need to take our medicine. Specifically, we need to take a humility pill. I call it our "inoculation."

## We Were The Enemy

In the Note to the Reader at the beginning of this book, I noted that every Christian was once an unbeliever. We need to remember from whence we came. If we don't start from that humble position, we will be crushed the first moment we flex our muscles in a feeble attempt to stand. The adversary is very clever, and before we get too far along in our discourse, he is sure to chop us down simply by tapping into our own self-doubts.

We have all found ourselves, from time to time, in a situation when all doubts come raining down. A time when we are no longer sure of ourselves or of anything that we have set out to accomplish.

In trying times like these, it is very important to look back and rediscover our origins. Where have we come from? We come from God, but we have been evil. We often incline our head in an intelligent pose, asking ourselves, "What is evil?" as if we were unfamiliar with the concept. In fact, we all have been intimately steeped in, and in collusion with, the father of evil, Satan himself. Who do we think we are fooling when we ask, "What is evil?" Have we forgotten what we once were? Do we not remember where we came from?

We need reminding. Paul (who was formerly "Saul of Tarsus," a relentless persecutor of early Christians before his conversion on the road to Damascus) is just the man to do the reminding. In Ephesians 2:1-3, Paul, inspired by the Holy Spirit, sets the record straight–lest we deceive ourselves:

*"1 And you were dead in your trespasses and sins,*

> 2 *in which you formerly walked according to the course of this world, according to the prince of the power of the air, of the spirit that is now working in the sons of disobedience.*
>
> 3 *Among them we too all formerly lived in the lusts of our flesh, indulging the desires of the flesh and of the mind, and were by nature children of wrath, even as the rest."*

## He Made Us Alive!

The first chapter of Ephesians recounts the many blessings God has bestowed upon us, particularly as they pertain to our redemption in Christ. In chapter two, Paul reminds us why this is so important by pointing out what a hopeless condition we were in prior to our redemption. In Ephesians 2:1 we are told, "And you were dead in your trespasses and sins."

Note that God *made* us alive because otherwise we were *dead* in our sins and transgressions. That's where we were, where we come from. The Greek word for *dead* here is usually interpreted as the eternal death resulting from our sin. But the context here gives the word a slightly different meaning, which we must distinguish if we are to truly remember where we came from, or more specifically, what we once were. The Greek word Paul uses for *dead* specifically means that we were unable to respond to any impulse or to perform any function (unable, ineffective, dead, powerless). We were unable to respond to matters relating to God because of our sins. We were spiritually dead, destitute of force or power, inactive, inoperative. In other words, this is not a traditional meaning limited only to bodily death but a sense of utter inability to respond to the things of God.

Note also that Paul uses both the words *transgressions* (or trespasses) and *sins*. The original Greek word for *trespass* means to literally *fall by the side*. It conveys a sense of stumbling, falling short, or being led away. Conversely, the Greek word for *sin* clearly conveys purposeful evil, wickedness, and inequity. Why did Paul employ both of these words? It may be that Paul is not making a distinction between those who clearly choose to do evil to fulfill their own lustful desires and those who are led away because they are not discerning. There seems to be no difference between the two in God's eyes. *Each is dead and unable to respond to the things of God.* Those of us who are led away by false prophets would appear to be in the same category as those who purposely set out to do evil. It seems then, that we have no excuse. Romans 1:18-20 makes this crystal clear.

Some of us were led astray, and some of us chose to purposely ignore and defy God. In each case, our actions led to our dead condition– unable to move, operate, or respond to God.

An old TV show episode I remember watching as a kid scared me to death. A patient in a hospital room, unable to move any part of her body, was left alone as both nurses on her floor accidentally left for the evening without informing the other. The patient lay there watching in horror as a huge spider spun its web directly over her head and began crawling toward her neck. The episode ended as the janitor passed by the door and flipped off the light switch without even looking into the room. This is the kind of dead Paul is describing. We were unable to move because our sin and trespasses had paralyzed us. We were literally stuck in the bed we made for ourselves with no way out.

Ephesians 2:2 continues this description and leaves no doubt of our former alliance:

> "2  in which you formerly walked according to the course (era, age) of this world, according to the prince (ruler) of the power of the air, of the spirit that is now working in the sons of disobedience."

*Parenthetical remarks are the author's, inserted for emphasis and clarity.*

Yes, we once walked that way. *Walk*, of course, means the conduct of our life, or our lifestyle. We hear much worldly validation of so-called "lifestyle choices" these days. We once fell for that line and walked according to the age of this world.

**The Prince Of The Air**

In the pagan world of New Testament times, many people believed that the nether-world spirits inhabited a plane between the earth and the heavens (thus "the air"). Paul is speaking of this belief to convey a very important message. Genesis tells us that Adam surrendered to Satan the power over an entire planet that God had given to man alone. When God gives something, he actually transfers ownership. The power and dominion over the earth was Adam's to do with as he chose, even as God commanded him to go forth, multiply, and subdue the earth. It was always Adam's choice to obey or disobey. From the time Adam surrendered his dominion of the earth until the present, Satan has been the ruler of his temporary domain.

Paul is saying in Ephesians 2:1-3 that Satan, the temporary ruler of this earth, ruled our lives before we were redeemed. As descendants of the disobedient Adam, each and every one of us has inherited that surrender of authority to Satan. The horror is this: by giving him that authority, we adopted Satan as our Father. Matthew 12:30 assures us that if we are not *with* God, we are most certainly *against* Him. What is worse, if we are not gathering for his Kingdom, we are scattering. There is no in-between, no place of innocence or neutrality within which we may hide.

Before you were saved, did you ever think of yourself as a Satan worshiper? No candles or dead cats and such? But you and I were indeed, by inheritance and by free choice, sons and daughters of Satan. So there we were, dead, unable to move or respond to anything of God.

Totally controlled by Satan, we walked in step with our times. And all the time we told ourselves we were such swell fellows!

It is important for us to remember that. We must remember how very lost and depraved we actually were and that we did not fully comprehend it. If we neglect this, we cannot see the unbeliever and his condition for what it is. If we do not understand the adversary, we cannot hope to stand up to him, much less reveal the truth to him.

When a Christian faces an unbeliever, it is like looking into a mirror he once owned. Dare we then gasp in indignation and desperation that we do not comprehend how "these people" can do the things they do? Of course we know their ways! And that understanding, that full knowledge of our adversary–his ways, means, methods, and most importantly his heart's intent–allows us to stand and engage with confidence. So let's admit up front our *former complete allegia*nce to our enemy Satan.

## The Sons of Disobedience

This same Satan now works in the Sons of Disobedience (Ephesians 2:2) who received their inheritance through Adam. The word "works" is the Greek word *energeo*. It means to function within, to be in action, to operate, to give energy. It makes sense that this is where we get our word "energy."

How does this apply to us? Something fuels us; we are never in a state of discharge and we cannot fuel ourselves. It would seem that if God does not energize us, we are unable to do anything related to Him. It follows then that, if God does not energize us and since we have no innate ability to energize ourselves, by definition we must be energized by Satan. Conversely, if God energizes us, we are dead to Satan. Either way, we are energized. As Sons of Disobedience, we were energized by Satan to do his bidding whether or not we want to face that fact.

Satan cannot work in the Sons of God, but only in the Sons of Disobedience. Those who are not of God are by default Satan's very own. Yes, we can succumb to momentary temptation, but if we belong to Christ, sooner rather than later we snap back. We still have to pay the worldly consequences of our sin.

However, the joyous news is that, once saved, we never lose our salvation. Why? We just said it. We can't stay separated; we will run back to the One who saves us because we are His and He is ours – forever. We are one in Christ, inseparable. Using an analogy given to us in scripture, it's like being married. This is why God hates divorce because marriage is an earthly (and therefore not perfect) model of our relationship with Christ. The binds of God's love, once man and Christ (or man and woman) are forged into one, can be stretched but cannot be broken.

But if we have not accepted Christ as our Savior, we are doomed forevermore to be sons of

Satan. We shall be his to torment for all eternity. These are very hard words indeed for those who have not accepted Christ. They most certainly make the Christian uncomfortable as they bring back a reminder of what we once were. Like the adversaries we face today, we did not see ourselves aligned with any power but our own. We did not realize that we were not, and never can be, our own. Satan is perfectly happy in the background where he doesn't have to answer any questions, to let you delude yourself into thinking that *you* are in control. Nevertheless, unbelievers belong to him heart and soul. Try to tell someone that he is deceived and you will hear human pride yell "Shields up!" That in-born reaction alone demonstrates that we are inherently evil, for otherwise our first reaction would be "Change course!"

## To The Heart Of The Matter: "But God..."

God is perfect; He is the blinding, searing light of good. Where God is, sin cannot exist. It is burned up, consumed in His presence. God and sin are like matter and anti-matter. This is why the wages of sin is death. Death is not some arbitrary punishment God assigned to sin. It is what must be if God is who He is. We became sin when Adam fell and therefore, we must die. We, like sin, were doomed to be consumed by the very presence of God.

But there is good news! Immediately after the fall, God put in place a plan for redemption (Genesis 3:15). What was this plan? How could we pay the penalty in order to be redeemed? The penalty is death. If we die an eternal death to pay for our sin, we cannot enjoy eternal life with God. God alone cannot pay the penalty because He is not guilty. But only God can pay the price and survive it because He cannot die. Still, we are left with the stark reality that the penalty must be paid. Sin must be consumed in God's presence. But who can pay it? Only someone who is both God and man is able to accomplish this.

Ephesians 2:1-3 paints a horrifying account of the impossible corner we allowed sin to back us into. How vicious is sin! What possible rescue could there be? Well, we are emerging now out of the darkness in this chapter into a most brilliant light. I present to you now a revelation that will take your breath away!

For it is certain that all of heaven gasped at two simple words that were eventually codified in verse 4: "***But God...***" – the two most precious words in scripture! Read it right now and be amazed! I guarantee you chills will run down your spine as you read the most pivotal passage in scripture. Ephesians 2:4-9 shatters the very teeth of the Evil one. It snatches us from darkness forever.

> "4 But God, being rich in mercy, because of His great love with which He loved us,
> 5 even when we were dead in our transgressions, made us alive together with Christ (by grace you have been saved),
> 6 and raised us up with Him, and seated us with Him in the heavenly places in Christ Jesus,
> 7 so that in the ages to come He might show the surpassing riches of His grace in kindness toward us in Christ Jesus.
> 8 For by grace you have been saved through faith; and that not of yourselves, it is the gift of God;
> 9 not as a result of works, so that no one may boast."

Imagine the sum total sins of your life and how they have incurred the wrath of God. Add to that the sins of all alive today who still refuse the gift of life that God has freely given. Then add to that the sins of all those souls who have lived before us throughout history. Finally, add to that the sins of all who will come after us, and you now begin to see the fully justified wrath of God. This mighty wrath was spent and exhausted once and for all on One whose body, every bone out of joint, hung on a splintered cross, soaked in His own precious blood. Utterly alone, He took on God's terrible wrath and paid the price for our sin once and for all. It is finished. It is over and done with. God's wrath is spent. Sin died where the blood fell.

Let us be eternally thankful there is a *"But God…"* in scripture. In this, the mother of all pivots in history, which side of *"But God…"* do you belong? Before we stand our ground against the adversary, we need to take a moment to rejoice in our rescue.

If we remember where we came from, we will not be caught off guard when the unbeliever pointedly reminds us. Instead, we will rejoice over our transformation in Christ. Now, not only do we remember our past, but also we know the present condition of those who seek to wipe God from the planet. They can keep no secrets from us because we already know everything about them. We know how they think. We know how they operate. We know their true motives and what drives them, for we were once them. We have a huge advantage over them, if only we use it.

## Your Inoculation

If you cannot come face-to-face with the fact that you (and I) were once evil and sons of Satan, you are not ready to stand against the adversary. Do every believer a favor and stay out of the battle until you have fully reconciled with your Savior. These are harsh words for some, but those who run out unprepared and unarmed do much damage to our God-given mission to bring true light into the world. We cannot be ready until we are first completely honest with ourselves. Once in that place, we are invincible and the enemy will have no hold over us.

If we try to skip over this inoculation, the unbeliever will certainly point out the fact that we have not been honest with ourselves, thus injuring our integrity. And down we then go, forever useless. Trust me and take the pill! It will inoculate you from any true charge of hypocrisy. It will clean you so that no speck may be found upon you as you stand directly in the path of the unbeliever. Think about your own life and how God has worked to rescue you from total darkness. How blessed are you! How very, very precious you are to Him!

As we bring to bear the mighty power of the Holy Spirit and prepare to stand against those who defy God, we must do so with an utterly bottomless humility. It is this same spirit with which the God of the universe, who had no guilt, emptied Himself upon the cross. By accepting Christ, we are *no longer guilty*. From the Christian, unburdened by guilt, blossoms a ferocious and unstoppable godly righteousness with which he embarks on a most sacred mission. Soon, the King of Kings will return in all His majesty and glory to claim us. Until that day, we have some work to do together.

## Chapter 5

# The Time For Action Has Come

It's all about action. Chapters one through four have set the table for the action that must follow if we are to take our stand. We talked about prayer as our first and last action. We learned a little bit about politics and religion as they relate to the proper battlefield upon which the Christian is to engage. We have asked ourselves, in the final analysis, what it is we fear that prevents us from taking action. And we have had a brutally frank discussion about where we Christians have come from, a remembrance that prods us into action. Now it's time to roll.

As we begin to map out an action plan, we will delve a little deeper into these previous subjects. We will discover how intricately they are woven into the fabric of Christian response. But I first want to stop and show you our current thinking. I said "Christian *response.*" A response is a reactive measure, not a proactive one. We have been in response mode for so long that many of us have no idea what it is like to live as a proactive Christian.

## Stand Where Our Faith Begins

Now here is the most radical proposition of this book: in taking our stand, Christians should NOT confine their response to the current political climate.

Why?

Because a response, by definition, meets the problem where it currently resides on a continuum. We have conceded so much ground that if we started with the meager bit we have retained, our message would be so watered down by liberalism that one would not be able to tell the difference between Christianity and the local Moose Lodge. [*Moose International is known throughout the world as a most noble and charitable organization, by the way.*]

For Christians to take a stand, we must first *return to stand where our faith begins*, not from the corner to which we have been pushed. Christians must fully demonstrate the radical contrast between Christianity and the world around us. The stark divide between our world-view and our world should be trumpeted in the public square. To help sustain us, we should all keep the prayer of Nehemiah in mind (Nehemiah 1:1-11).

We must express, as did Nehemiah, our heartfelt sorrow for the sins our nation has committed. Then we must ask God for His mercy to change the course of our nation. You may think to yourself, "Well, I'm not depraved, they are!" Yet since "they" reside in the dark and will not pray, we must pray for them. This is our priestly role. For we know God while they do not. And since we, too, are of this nation, we must include ourselves in that call to repentance. We want our nation to recover from its tears when the Gospel is heard, as though for the first time (Nehemiah 8:9). For nothing is beyond God, and He has shown that He can certainly bring about a monumental repentance, if the nation is willing. But first, it must know the depths of its depravity.

We are not going to change this country by directly addressing political issues of the day. If we start from today's mindset, we would have to spend years working our way back to primary biblical principles. Because of the snowballing momentum of the unbeliever, we would never get there.

Of course we should be politically active and work hard in our communities to elect and support those who share our values. Those values are already codified in the Constitution to the extent any representative republic can contain them. Most state constitutions are similar to our federal Constitution. In our states we have the same power as we do on the federal level and should wield every ounce of it. As Christians, we are already working hard in our communities to affect favorable political outcomes throughout the political spectrum, and we should continue to do so. But as we have seen over the last six to ten years, it's not enough.

## Political Parties And Our Vote

Christians in the United States are continually outvoted. We need to ask ourselves why this is so and work to understand what we can do to reverse the situation. To begin, let's take another quick look at the current political climate in the United States.

We enjoy what is essentially a two-party system in this country. This is a very general statement, of course. I would ask the reader to accept this very broad premise for the sake of our immediate context. Democrats and Republicans have duked it out for years in a never-ending pendulum swing. It is true that most Christians are politically conservative and therefore usually vote with the conservative party – the Republicans, but that is never a given. It is also true that the 2014 midterm election went well for Republicans. But look what the nation had to experience before it would effectively switch parties, at least temporarily. And what guarantee is there that the Republican Party will fare any better than the other party?

We can have no definitive discussion about Independents, or even the Tea Party, because their viability flows into, rather than alongside, the stream of the two major parties. For instance, voters in the 2014 Kansas midterm election were left scratching their heads when presented with an Independent running against an incumbent Republican for the cherished Senate seat. Both major parties viewed the Kansas seat as key to overturning power in the Senate. The Democrat had dropped out, apparently believing an Independent would soundly defeat a weak Republican incumbent if a Democrat were not also in the race syphoning off votes. Independent Greg Orman's run crystalizes the inherent problem with the so-called "Independent Party." Republicans unmasked Orman as a Democrat while the Democratic Vice President promptly claimed Orman as the Democratic party's adopted son. Orman, a political orphan, couldn't articulate whom he would vote with on any given issue. In the end, Kansas voters decided against the enigmatic independence of Greg Orman for the certainly Republican Pat Roberts. Ironically, while incumbent Pat Roberts suffered from a chronically low favorability rating across the entire state, he won by a wide margin over a declared Independent.

The Republican establishment, bruised from running unpolished and unsuccessful Tea Party candidates under the Republican banner in 2012, pre-empted any real Tea Party challenge in 2014 through a brutal and sometimes nasty elimination program during the primaries. They could do this because there is no Tea Party. They all register and run as Republicans or Independents – so far.

Certainly Independents wield influence. Tea Party activists strongly impact the political landscape as well, especially within the Republican Party. There are a host of other registered parties, but even with the current resurgence of the Libertarian Party, none seriously compete with the two main parties on the national level. This may change, but any shift would only lead to a different two-party system, even if only momentarily. So once in office, a candidate from any party, real or imagined, votes either with Republicans or with Democrats on any given issue. An "Independent" voter is no longer independent when he comes out of that polling booth and neither is the independent candidate for whom he voted. The sweet cotton candy of political "independence" always dissolves in the wet and sticky mouth of decision.

Our history tells us we can temporarily work with more than two parties, but the equilibrium always forces a binary choice. This actually mirrors science and humanity where every mathematical problem, every social issue, and every election literally comes down to a choice between one or the other of two possible outcomes.

Recently, Republicans have *responded* to Democrats from the current philosophical starting point on the political map. That point is very far back from true conservatism. With each election, Republicans have allowed themselves to be pushed back further. Worse, with each subsequent election they start from that further point back. In the 2014 midterm elections, Republicans didn't even bother to articulate a philosophical starting point. In that election, voters overwhelmingly voted against the party in power, not for any articulated Republican philosophy. In the end, it becomes difficult for a voter to discern any real difference between Democrat and Republican. The conservative message in the Republican Party becomes more and more diluted as they start from a point further back from the previous election (assuming they even bother to articulate a message).

**How Easy It Is To Go Astray**

How easy is it for the Christian to be led astray by politics? Let's just take one obvious example: the Bible assures us that both men and women are equal before God but different in their roles. There is no inequality between man and woman before God. We have only to look back all the way to Genesis chapters two and three to see very clearly their complementary roles. We do not compete with each other; we were made to complement each other, becoming one with each other through our separate roles before God. Yet Satan whispers that we are somehow being cheated out of our personal greatness. If a man abandons his natural role, the intended fruit of that role rots on the tree and God's will is temporarily thwarted. More importantly, many blessings meant for that man are never realized. Similarly, if a woman decides to exchange her role for a man's biblical role, what was meant for her and all that depended on her original role goes unfulfilled. Who takes her place? Something, somewhere, goes undone.

In our world today, in cooperation with Satan, both genders are blurred beyond recognition and the children of the world are suffering for it, especially those conceived and growing in the womb. Certainly roles overlap at times, but we are talking about wholesale role exchanges, if not outright role abandonment. If the Christian does not stand in the face of such apostasy, he walks according to the "prince of the air" and not according to God. How many professed Christians do you know have surrendered their vigilance of this primary biblical principle of gender equality in exchange for what the world calls "gender equality?"

That's how easy it is to go astray, and it stems from a lack of biblical knowledge. Biblical ignorance steps into the knowledge gap to dull the senses and acts as a fertilizer for tares in God's wheat field. These weeds, born of the unbeliever's religion, spread their way onto the unbeliever's political battlefield.

In the 2014 midterm election, one political party manufactured a mythical "war on women." Much of their polemics centered on the premise that women are solely interested in a "divinely" inherited right to murder the baby in their wombs if they want to. Apparently for that political party, women exist only for this "choice." They have no other interests. Thankfully, an educated electorate rejected this attempt to pit woman against man and mother against child. Remember that the fundamental goal of Satan is to set one person against another, to divide and conquer that which God intends to be whole (man, woman, child, family). Certain political parties excel at this technique, dividing the nation by building up artificial separators, setting us all against each other for their personal power and profit. And while we are all busy scratching and biting at each other, they seize power for themselves. Yes, that is how easy it is to go astray.

**Drawing A Stark Contrast**

I think anyone can see by now that placing our hope in any particular political party is not the answer. Remember that the political realm is the battlefield of the unbeliever. Our battlefield is spiritual. We are first igniting a prairie fire in this country that will burn in the hearts of our countrymen. Only then will the ballot box catch fire. But first we must win back hearts and minds.

I would note, however, that if conservatives actually adopted the process we Christians are adopting in our stand, this country would see a prairie fire of conservatism. It's been done before. This is exactly what Ronald Reagan did in 1976 and in 1980. He did not accept the false axiom that Republicans needed to start from the corner Jimmy Carter and the Democrats had pushed them to. Instead, Reagan boldly packaged the top tenants of true conservatism into a message that appeared to be so radical to the downtrodden Republican Party; it lit a fire that burned for the next 12 years. In fact, that message was not radical at all but was simply a restatement of true conservative values that had not changed since their inception. They just seemed radical because of the progressive degradation of those values that had slowly, but significantly, changed the political landscape over the Ford and Carter years. As a result, Reagan won two consecutive electoral landslides the likes of which we have not seen since.

Imagine Christians doing the same thing! Imagine not starting our stand with a three-layer-deep argument on whether homosexuality is genetically induced, for instance. Imagine not attempting to stem the tide of abortion by simply trying to reverse compulsory subsidies for abortion in the Affordable Care Act. What if we started from our first principles? We would appear quite radical, but that startling contrast is what induces change. Milquetoast incrementalism moves nothing. We need to begin with the Bible, not from our present position on the unbeliever's progressive continuum.

In the Introduction, you may recall I started each sentence with "There was a time when..." and then drew a series of stark contrasts to today. From now on, when people see us, they need to see that bold difference. Many people are fond of saying, "These days, there is no modesty, no shame." Shame only becomes visible as light contrasts with darkness, silhouetting the vivid reality of biblical truth against the perpetual deceit that shades our eyes. But if there is no light, there can be no contrast.

Without realizing it, we have watered down our "essence of Christ" in order to avoid constant controversy. I have some startling news: to many, *Christ is confrontation*. Confrontation, however, brings about reconciliation. The Gospel strives to point out the dire need of the salvation Christ offers. If we do not illuminate the vivid contrast of the whole Gospel against the backdrop of sin before the eyes of unbelievers, we do not carry the cross before us. Rather, we carry a white flag.

From here on, unbelievers will view us as radicals. That might cause some to cringe, but let me ask you a question. When did unbelievers consider us anything else *but* radicals? Even when we try to be more and more like them, the meager resistance we offer is labeled "extremist." Christians will always be attacked and ridiculed. That doesn't matter. What does matter is our faithfulness to our Lord. We stand on first principles, and it's time the world heard from us with one united voice.

**We Shall Fear No Longer**

Therefore, that which God has spoken to us in the darkness, during our intimacy with Him, we must speak out in the light of day. We shall no longer fear confrontation. Whatever He has whispered into our ears, we must shout from the rooftops (Matthew 10:26-27). Yes, some of us, your author included, may feel some humiliation that this realization has been a long time in coming. If you're like me, you might be a little perturbed that we have been slow in understanding what He was telling us. But we have heard our Lord now and can step up into the light, carry that cross, and take exceeding joy in knowing He is with us. Amen!

No pussyfooting around now. If we are going to take our stand, we are going to have to go all the way. We can no longer be lukewarm, for He hates this (Revelation 3:13). We can no longer seek the grey area and call it "compassion." We can no longer avoid controversy and call it "striving for unity." We cannot relieve the unbeliever's constant hydraulic pressure by simply claiming, "We are all Children of God." That is *not* true. Unbelievers are *not* Children of God. They have another Father, and we know who he is.

**The True Children Of God**

Scripture clearly tells us that only those who have received Christ were given the right to be called Children of God (John 1:12-13). Remember the context of this passage. God the Logos (The Word, Christ) was in the world, which was made through Him, but the world just did not want to know Him. But those who did were given an extraordinary right and authority to be grafted into His royal family, permanently adopted as Sons of God (Romans

11:17-18). Every branch grafted onto the tree is supported by the root and is in every way an integral part of the tree. That's you and me! Those who have not accepted Christ reject the root, have no sustainment from that root, and are not an integral part of God's family. They must, by definition, wither and die.

I spent much of my childhood and teen years in and out of foster homes. In a sense, I was "adopted" into those families. Trust me, you never, ever walk as one with them. No matter how hard any loving adopted family tries to graft you in, the grafting scar is always visible as a reminder. It's not for lack of trying; it just isn't humanly possible if the child has memories of his own family. Some families tried hard, others did not. I am blessed to have adopted brothers and sisters I fellowship with to this day, while others I never saw again. But in every case I always knew I was the outsider, even though that was not fair to them. I *was* blessed to have one family where I was as close to a son as can be. But, in mourning for my broken family, there was still a gap. But this was all good because it taught me to depend on God, the one constant in our lives. It built character. I am very grateful to every one of those families who took me in, loved me, sacrificed much, and called me their own – if only for a time. But even the best earthly adoptions can only mimic God's perfect adoption.

The adoption John and Paul write about, inspired by the Holy Spirit, is nothing like an earthly adoption. It is a permanent and physical grafting onto the olive tree, as it were. God's grafting leaves no visible evidence to mark our adoption. We are His and He is ours absolutely and completely. Human adoption is imperfect. Godly adoption is absolutely complete and perfect. Therefore we must not be flippant with scripture by ascribing attributes to God that actually have nothing to do with Him. Unbelievers are NOT Children of God.

God loves everyone, but not everyone is His. When the time comes, there will be much wailing and gnashing of teeth as those who had falsely convinced themselves they were His are reminded otherwise (Matthew 7:21-23). Note the context here. This rejection by Christ is directly based on action – those who *did His will* and those who did not. The Gospel is action, belief is action, faith is action, and, thank God, grace is action. Our call to stand is also a call to action. We can't just "feel" and opine our way into changing the world. The Gospel requires us to *do*. The time for action has come.

## A Prayer To Action

In the past we have heard many people say, "First we will pray, then we will act." We know what they mean, but we must understand with all certainty that heartfelt prayer *is action*. On the other hand, many feel that, if they have prayed earnestly, they have acted. If that is all they can do, yes, they have acted. If we can do more, we start with prayer and proceed to go as far as God will allow.

So let us start with prayer.

*Father, we know that you are on Your throne and that You are sovereign over the entire world. Nothing happens without Your sovereign authority. We know that Your ways are not our ways. We come together today as one, on our knees before You. We ask You to empower us, by the power of the Holy Spirit, to stand in Your holy name against the powers and principalities of this world. Above all, let us stand as one, united in Your name in complete obedience to Your will. Let Your Word, the power of the Gospel, penetrate hardened hearts where no mere human can go. We pray for a time of great revival, where Your Word reigns supreme, shining a searing light in the darkness around us. May Your light pierce the hearts and minds of many and heal our nation. In the name of the Father, the Son, and the Holy Spirit we beseech You with all of our heart, mind, body and soul. Amen.*

## Chapter Six

# Judgment or Discernment? – The Example of the Pharisees

"How dare you judge me? Jesus said 'Judge not lest ye be judged,' and you call yourself a Christian? You don't even know your own Bible!"

Well now, don't I feel silly? I guess that's the last time I try to take a stand. I reluctantly back off, stunned into thinking somehow I'm a hypocrite. But I'm also thinking something just got by me there. In the back of my mind, I know something is wrong with that "judge not" argument. I just can't quite put my finger on it.

So let's put our finger on it.

## The Scripture Twisters

As we take our stand, we should function as a rock-solid lighthouse, deeply anchored in firm biblical ground, illuminating the darkness. This spotlight on sin makes it clear that we collectively are not going to participate in the unbeliever's agenda, nor will we stand by as that agenda destroys our country. Together, we are going to resist any effort to turn our nation further away from God. We are not going to retreat. Instead, we will begin to turn our nation back toward Him. As soon as we stand up to do this, we will hear the familiar refrain, "How dare you judge me!"

The unbeliever is attempting to use the Bible, the very basis of our faith and call to action, against us. This is not the first time this has been done. Satan used this old trick on the Son of God. While tempting Christ, the Father of All Lies manipulated scripture into false arguments. But in each case, Jesus replied, "It is also written..." in order to return the twisted scripture into its proper context (Matthew 4:1-11). This is what we must do as well.

When unbelievers piously admonish us that we should not judge, they are executing the greatest flimflam of all time on the Bible. The tempting illusion they proffer is that we are relieved from the burden of sin because we are not qualified to "judge." They falsely and automatically characterize as "judgment" any proper discernment utilized by the Christian to detect and recognize sin. This is an utterly false notion and a gross misapplication of scripture.

In the seventh chapter of Matthew, during the Sermon on the Mount, Jesus delegates to us the authority to discern sin from righteousness, both in our own lives and in others'. In doing so, He leaves no excuse for allowing ourselves to be led away from the faith. Earlier in chapter seven, as He warns us that the Judgment Seat is not ours to inhabit, He also declares that we should ensure we are innocent *before* we point out the sins of others (Matthew 7:1-5). Therefore, under the conditions He sets for us, *we are to point out the sins of others*. The purpose of such an action is to demonstrate to the world the need for repentance and forgiveness. The Great Commission in Matthew 28:19-20 compels us to teach the world all that Christ commanded. Our obedience to this ordinance serves a singular purpose – to point out our desperate need for salvation.

## Judgment Or Discernment?

So what is the difference between judgment and discernment? Throughout the New Testament, the Greek word used here for "judge" is almost exclusively used in the legal sense. Someone in authority "judges" an action by another and imposes, either explicitly or implicitly, a sentence. There are variations throughout the New Testament of course, but they are always well bounded by this sense of legality.

Rarely is this word used in the more general sense, especially as we understand it in English, as "to believe" or to "decide one way or another." Nor is the word confused with discernment as we English speakers do: "Bill *judged* that the slam of the door provided a strong indication it would not open again soon." The Greek word for "judge" in the seventh chapter of Matthew connotes a strong sense of the actor being the accuser, judge and jury. The lesson is that Satan is the accuser; God is the judge and jury. We should not be any of these things.

There is a real difference between pointing out the need for salvation and accusing a person of being condemned to hell for all eternity. We are not the ones who send them there and we do not know with certainty how God will determine where they spend eternity. We can, however, employ biblical discernment and perform "what if" scenarios, if you will. We can say, for instance, that *if* they are not saved, and *if* they continue down their current path until the day they die, we know for certain how God will judge them. He has told us in no uncertain terms (Matthew 7:13-14, Romans 6:23, Mark 9:43-48, et al). But we are not omniscient. We do not *know* this person's future and we are not qualified to hit the fast forward button on the remote control of their lives. This is solely God's jurisdiction, not ours. We, on the other hand, are to carry out Matthew 28:19-20 and leave the rest to the Holy Spirit.

Now, does this mean we are not allowed to point out sin? Of course it doesn't! But let us first point out our own sin, get ourselves right with God, and then we can take on the world. Only after we have taken care of our own propensity for sin can we help anyone else. That is why prayer is always our first action.

The question is, how do we get to that place where we can distinguish righteousness from sin?

We all have an innate ability to differentiate the two. However, because of our unbounded propensity to rationalize sin into false righteousness, it is no coincidence that the line is so often blurred. This is called relativism, a philosophical term describing the manipulation of truth relative to one's desired outcome. Today, relativism runs rampant whereby every individual manufactures his own right and wrong "definitionizer." But it doesn't work when interacting with other people, and it doesn't work inside our own individual consciences.

Suppose I feel I have a right to let my dog run free. After all, I might believe animals have rights too, that I should not confine an animal as it amounts to cruelty by stripping the animal of its natural instincts. You, my neighbor, may have a completely different view of what is right and true in this situation. In the meantime, I have a new neighbor move in up the street. He believes as I do. The trouble is, *his dog* is all over *my lawn* and threatening me if I go outside. I might change my mind about what is right and wrong, true or false. Or, I might even condemn my new neighbor by some contrivance while maintaining my own right to let my dog roam. Whatever relative path I take, the result is a messy, confused, and angry neighborhood.

We often change our mind depending upon each situation we face. The "truth" changes frequently for each individual relativist and is not shared across individuals. There is no overarching truth to appeal to. Either way you look at it, relativism doesn't work, period. It is the path to anarchy.

If you understand that analogy, there's more. Christians are actually being judged under the relativism of the unbeliever when they charge us with "judging"; and we are certainly allowed under the rules of their game to counter the charge. We can certainly argue that they have no right to "judge that we were judging them." But then, of course, they can charge us with "judging them for judging us for judging them." You see how silly it gets when we depart from God's truth. Unbelievers often back themselves into logic corners like this. We often don't take two minutes to recognize they just trapped themselves. If we center on Christ, we will see unbelievers for who they are, and we will recognize that they have not pushed us into a corner. Instead, they have placed themselves in that corner with no way out, if we decide to point it out. And we should. Every time. That is, as long as we are settled up with God.

So it is clear that the Bible refers to judgment as the act of determining guilt and passing sentence, whereas discernment is the innate ability to determine sin from righteousness. Much of the unbeliever's problem stems from the fact that he does not *know* the Bible. Yet this same unbeliever *judges* the Bible. The key words in Matthew 7 are "judge" and "know." It is from the first part of this chapter the unbeliever accuses us:

## Judging Others

"1 Do not judge so that you will not be judged.
2 "For in the way you judge, you will be judged; and by your standard of measure, it will be measured to you.
3 "Why do you look at the speck that is in your brother's eye, but do not notice the log that is in your own eye?
4 "Or how can you say to your brother, 'Let me take the speck out of your eye,' and behold, the log is in your own eye?
5 "You hypocrite, first take the log out of your own eye, and then you will see clearly to take the speck out of your brother's eye."

The unbeliever purposely ignores the passage below, which closely follows the passage on judgment. This second passage in Matthew 7 commands us all to discern between sin and righteousness:

## A Tree and Its Fruit

> "15 Beware of the false prophets, who come to you in sheep's clothing, but inwardly are ravenous wolves.
> 16 "You will know them by their fruits. Grapes are not gathered from thorn bushes nor figs from thistles, are they?
> 17 "So every good tree bears good fruit, but the bad tree bears bad fruit.
> 18 "A good tree cannot produce bad fruit, nor can a bad tree produce good fruit.
> 19 "Every tree that does not bear good fruit is cut down and thrown into the fire.
> 20 "So then, you will know them by their fruits."

In this companion passage, Jesus teaches us how to discern false prophets from true prophets. In today's vernacular, Jesus is showing us how we can tell whether a person is honest or sinful. Essentially, we can tell by the fruit he bears in his life. In a very real sense, we are to discern actions from words, deeds from intent, results from promises.

This is biblical discernment. Jesus declares that we should not *judge* and then closely follows that up with instructions by which we will *know* a false prophet. The Greek word for "know" here translates directly to the English word "knowledge." There is no mistaking Our Lord's point; judgment leads to sin while discernment leads to knowledge. And knowledge leads to righteousness.

By this we know if we are dealing with a wolf in sheep's clothing or with the genuine article. One has to recognize sin in order to avoid it and admonish against it. This is how we are instructed to recognize sin in a deceitful world. You can lie with words, but actions and results are undeniably obvious for all to see. In fact, many people today are beginning to use this biblical principle in determining the veracity of the politicians whom they place in office.

## The Example Of The Pharisees

In Matthew 7:15-20, Jesus was addressing both the Pharisees specifically and discernment in general. As usual, He chose the perfect example. The Pharisees of Jesus' time, in their interaction with their own people and the government of Rome, provide an extended example of unintended consequences and why the biblical practice of discernment is crucial. It is worth taking a little time to travel back into history so that we can then see the parallels to our own time.

The Pharisees of the first century were not only religious leaders; they were also political leaders who had, over time, sold their party out to the Herodians and others who had no connection with the faith of the Jewish people. A classic example of that sellout is the "trial" of Jesus, initiated by the Pharisees but completed by the State of Rome. The Pharisees made Jesus a political "hot potato" by accusing him of sedition against Rome (He claimed to be a king). Actually, the Pharisees were more concerned that Jesus' perceived blasphemy threatened to usurp their dearly held political power. They decided that the only way to silence Him and his followers was to kill Him. Since it was forbidden under Roman rule for the Pharisees to execute anyone, they turned Jesus over to King Herod. Herod, a weak leader caught between the religious power wielded by the Pharisees and Rome's geopolitical might, handed Jesus off to the Roman procurator, Pontius Pilot, in hopes that Pilot would execute Jesus and placate the Pharisees.

This King Herod was the son of the Edomite half-caste Herod The Great. Ironically, both of these kings were regarded as unfit by their bloodline to rule over the Jews. Politics does indeed make strange bedfellows.

Pilot was reluctant to execute Jesus because, under Roman law, the crime did not warrant the Roman punishment of death. Pilot, constrained by his office, could not choose which Roman laws to enforce or ignore, nor could he pronounce a sentence the law did not allow. With their very political survival at risk if Jesus survived this trial, the Pharisees went for broke.

They took advantage of a Roman amnesty custom that Pilot had hoped would relieve him of having to execute Jesus. But the Pharisees, whose power was rooted in their ability to mobilize the people, ginned up the crowd to force the release of a convicted criminal rather than release Jesus. Through diabolical political trickery, they strove to squeeze an illegal Roman execution order out of the reluctant Pilot. The implicit threat by the Pharisees, if they did not get their way, was to bring about a massive riot resulting in chaos and destruction to the streets of Jerusalem and threatening the very government of Rome. They used the people, who lacked discernment in their crowd mentality, to threaten violence and disobedience against Rome. Pilot understood all too well this very real threat of mob-rule as he witnessed the huge crowd inexplicably reject his offer of amnesty for Jesus. If he did not acquiesce, the resulting anarchy would forever destroy Pilot's career in the eyes of Rome.

Shamefully, the Pharisees threatened their own people, whom they were supposed to protect and govern, and used them to incite chaos to get their way. The Pharisees, it would seem, had chosen politics as their political battleground. Their trifecta attack pitting the Jewish people against the synagogue (the Pharisee leaders), while pitting the weak King Herod against Rome, represented an exquisite triangular political dilemma in which the Pharisees were well practiced.

The whole trial, from start to finish, was an illegal sham. The Pharisees cashed in all of their political chips at once. It was now all or nothing. From beginning to end, it was pure and malicious evil against the very people they were sworn to serve. The legal precedent and surrender of Jewish sovereignty they set that day (Roman execution of their own people) was scandalous. They manipulated their own Sanhedrin judges, the court of the Jewish king, and most insidiously, the court of Rome. They illegally rigged all three in one way or another to get their way. The Pharisees no longer had any regard for the preservation of the Jewish nation. They committed high treason against their own nation, pulling out all the stops in a desperate attempt to keep their own party in power at all costs. Does this sound familiar today? Also, don't overlook the example of poor discernment exercised by the people, who collectively were the actual tool of power. Without the people, manipulated as they were, the Pharisees could do nothing.

Although beyond the scope of this book, Pilot is an interesting study. His discernment was dead on, but although empowered by his government to deliver judgment over the province, he exercised it poorly. It isn't like Pilot didn't have any warning. Even his own wife, with whom biblically he was one, strongly warned him against being manipulated by the Pharisees against an innocent man. We can take away at least three lessons from his actions in history.

First, as with our situation today, he had foolishly allowed himself to be slowly backed into a corner. Secondly, he chose his own political survival over the life of an innocent man. Thirdly, and perhaps most egregiously, he attempted to manufacture false distance between himself and his own actions. Though he may have washed his hands, they are, to this day, dripping with the blood of the only totally innocent human in history. Pilot is a lesson in vigilance against the serious consequences of political expediency.

It is often said that sin takes you farther than you ever intended to go. The Pharisees' treachery knew no end. They even conspired with the very guard they procured from Pilot to guard the tomb of Christ (Matthew 28:11-15). Well aware that Jesus had said that He would rise again after three days, they begged Pilot to post a Roman guard at the tomb. Siding with Herod, injecting the hated Romans into the private Jewish legal system, and intimidating their own people was bad enough, but now they saw a new problem that had them slipping deeper and deeper into hypocrisy.

Since the risen Christ left an embarrassingly empty tomb in the presence of an entire armed Roman guard contingent, both the Pharisees and the Roman guard had some explaining to do. The Pharisees promised the Roman guard, traditionally about a half dozen soldiers, that they would square it for them with Pilot. So they struck a deal.

The guards would lie and say that Jesus' disciples (who had, in reality, scattered throughout the land since the trial) came in the middle of the night to steal the body from a heavily sealed tomb while the entire armed guard slept through an earthquake. In return, the Pharisees paid the soldiers handsomely for this ridiculous farce (Matthew 28:15). They had to, since the hastily concocted story did not even approach the edge of believability and the penalty for failure of a Roman guard unit was death. But the last thing the Pharisees wanted was for the soldiers to corroborate the disciples' account of the resurrection.

Scripture does not record the further misadventures of these Keystone Kops, but there were only two options remaining to them, considering Roman history in Judea at the time. It is likely the entire Roman guard either deserted soon after the Pharisees paid them, or Pilot executed them. Choosing to disregard the truth for the sake of political expediency, they were all backed into an inescapable corner because of their deceit and lack of proper discernment.

Travel now with me back to the present day. Observe the current political landscape. Nothing has changed. We see unbelievers doing the same thing. Such is the cost of the perversion of truth. Political parties sell out their own "people" for political prizes, and the people, lacking discernment, follow right along.

The Pharisees claimed the mantle had been handed down to them from the Levite Priests from Mosaic Law. But they had perverted it by adding greatly to it over the years. Their constant fiddling with scripture had placed the people under an unnecessarily heavy burden, locking them into dilemma after dilemma. Today, as well, our laws are beginning to lock the Christian into dilemma after dilemma.

Scripture records an entire chapter's worth of narrative by Jesus, his harshest attack yet, on this very serious problem (Matthew 23). The Pharisees had gained concentrated political power for a tiny few. These elite few banned together and privately (and sometimes openly) claimed to be above the people. They enjoyed many luxuries, the best spots in the synagogue, the "respect" of the entire community, immense political power, and the fear of their own people. I ask again, does this sound familiar today?

Jesus had come to fulfill the law, which had provided no escape from the wages of sin. At the same time, He rescued us from its merciless consequences (Romans 6:23). Simultaneously, Jesus upheld the law, fulfilled the law, and rescued us from the law. This is a truly marvelous conundrum to those who do not understand Jesus and his work on the cross. Even as the law was laid down, God had told His people He desires mercy, not rote sacrifice (Hosea 6:6, Matthew 9:13, 12:7).

The deleterious impact of the Pharisees on the people was not just spiritual; it exacted a huge economic toll as well. Through their political power over the people, the Pharisees demanded for themselves temple taxes, sacrificial rituals, and veneration. Nearly every economic action had come under the control of the Pharisees. They placed a heavy surtax by requiring everyone to change their local currency into temple currency in order to carry out the *required* sacrifice at the *required* location, which the Pharisees and their political allies owned, operated, and controlled. They were in the business of handing out judgment, not mercy, and they did so at a handsome profit.

Unbelievers invariably try to represent Jesus as always meek, gentle, and loving to every human being during His time on Earth. They conveniently forget that twice He took a whip to those who had turned His Father's house (the temple) into a "den of thieves" (Matthew 21:13, Mark 11:17, Luke 19:46). These recorded events provide a glimpse into the triumphant Jesus who is returning soon.

**"...I Never Knew you..."**

So we have come full circle in understanding the difference between judgment and discernment. We have seen how the poor exercise of judgment and discernment enslaved the people to their political leaders. In turn, we have seen that such power, once gained over the people, corrupts absolutely. The Christian, therefore, is charged with exercising proper discernment so that *he will not* be deceived. This requires real action on the part of the Christian. No Christian can excuse himself from the responsibility of discernment wherever and whenever he happens upon deception in his daily life. This is true whether it be in the news, from his next-door neighbor, his church, or his elected representatives. We must exercise discernment courageously, stand up and expose deception, and boldly counter with the truth. If we do not, we allow the lost to ride an air-conditioned train of deception all the way to their destruction.

Jesus warned that many Pharisees, though currently conspiring for His death, would on the Day of Judgment claim they were on His side all along (Matthew 7:21-22, 23:30). In that day our Lord would not recognize them. Jesus warned against playing both sides of the fence because the Pharisees were poisonous to the precious relationship between God and His people.

Christians, similarly, cannot play both sides of the fence. We are either with Him, and all that implies, or we are against Him (Matthew 12:30).

Jesus taught us, in the very same chapter in which He warned us about judgment, how to recognize these false prophets. We do not pass sentence upon those whom we know to be sinners. Instead, we are to teach them all that Jesus commanded. If they refuse to listen and to heed God's Word, we are to have nothing to do with them (Mathew 10:14, Mark 6:11, Luke 9:5). We are not to place them in a position of authority over us, as with the Pharisees in Jesus' time. They are not to have a place at our table, in our homes and churches, nor are we to take up their ways and consort with them. Notice that I said, "If they refuse." We are not excused from trying to reach them, simply because we *think* they will not listen.

We are charged by God to remain Christian and to share the good news with all who want to hear it. In no way are we obedient if we give up the ground Christ entrusted to us and allow sinners to rule over us, if we can prevent it.

**We Have Every Right**

Such a manifesto leaves us no option but to acknowledge the following:

We have every right, and are charged by Jesus Himself, to determine whether sin is present, recurrent or prevalent. We have every right to point out sin. We have every right to stand against sin with all that we are and all that God has given us. We have every right to be who we are and to stand our ground. We have every right to discern right from wrong and to assert right against wrong. Unbelievers are going to do what they will, but as for us, we shall follow the Lord (Joshua 24:15). This passage in Joshua outlines the responsibility of the believer to bring the unbeliever to decision point. That is what the Gospel is all about. We must never forget that these rights of ours are inalienable and God-given, directly authorized in God's Word and, not coincidentally, repeated in the Constitution of the United States of America.

Thus, we are always to be found active in service to our Lord. If we snooze while unbelievers assume their authoritative control over us, we lose.

The next time an unbeliever tells you that you have no right to judge, it is your Christian duty to immediately set that person straight; do not let the opportunity pass. If we are to stand on biblical truth, we must exercise biblical discernment. We have no choice but to determine the character and heart of others by the only reliable evidence available to us – the fruit they bear.

Unbelievers' hearts are hardened by years of deafness to the truth of God's Word, love, mercy, and grace. They do this, as we once did, to satisfy their own earthly desires. Sadly, those desires can never be satisfied. As hearts harden, it becomes more difficult to allow God in to fill a place only He can fill. If He is not in there to fill it, it remains an empty galactic black hole that the sinner vainly attempts to fill with anything and everything of this world.

The hardened heart is trained to resist God, who ironically is the only One who can soften and then fill it. However, there is a way to break this cycle…

# Chapter Seven

# The Hardened Heart

The Christian either lays "just another brick in the wall" of the hardened heart or he launches the catapult by which the Holy Spirit breaches that wall.

In ancient times, well before Alexander the Great, military engineers first sought to understand how a particular wall was constructed before they would devise a method to breach it. Similarly, understanding the construction of the hardened heart is a crucial step in our mission to stand. Remember we are standing so that no more ground shall be given. We will then march our way across whatever "neutral" ground remains and then fully engage the unbeliever. Recall that because the political battlefield is not the real one, *we cannot change elections until voters change their hearts*. The spiritual battlefield, within which the hardened heart is bunkered, is our challenge.

## Stand Faithful

Only God can bring about the required transformation, if we stand faithful. We cannot alter men outwardly; rather, we must bring change to their hearts through the power of the Holy Spirit. Put another way, we don't attack men; we pierce their hearts with the Gospel through the power of the Holy Spirit. How, you might ask? There is only one way. The truth must be told. If we do not, at every turn, speak the truth against the lie, how will any heart even consider the need for change?

At any time we decide to be silent, whether aided by a pleasant rationale for prudence or by easing our conscience by believing the truth we utter will fall on deaf ears, we aid and abet the enemy. So, unpleasant though it may sometimes be, we must always counter a lie *on the spot* with the truth. This is the only way a hardened heart can be changed by the Holy Spirit. If we do this every time, one-by-one, and together across our nation, hearts will be revived. Only then, with renewed hearts, will the political landscape of this country change. And once done, our nation will return to God.

The task requires radical action on the spiritual battlefield. As we have noted, this is no time to be "seeker sensitive." We must act in a way that suddenly and dramatically brings to mind the countless blessings this great nation has lost because of our unfaithfulness. We must lift the fog of ignorance and clearly show the dramatic contrast between the original foundation of our nation and what we have become. The dire straits in which we find ourselves will then be fully visible to everyone. This will then bring to mind the terrible abandonment and judgment that hovers over us. Our nation must be brought to tears, then to its knees in prayer, and finally to its feet to action. Only the Gospel, through the infinite power of the Holy Spirit, can do this. You might notice that this is the same confession-repentance-salvation pattern each believer has already passed through. It's inescapable if we are to reach out and grasp the free gift of salvation while it is still available. But, oh, what sweetness on the other side!

In this winter of our nation's soul, you might think this is impossible. By man's effort alone, I think I would agree with you; but with God, all things are possible (Matthew 19:26). It can be done. *It has been done before.*

## One Man Made The Difference

Travelling back in time to 640-609 BC, we marvel at the miraculous turnabout in Judah led by its young king Josiah. Josiah took over the reins of the kingdom at the tender age of eight. A dramatic history preceded Josiah's reign. Upon the death of Solomon, Israel (The Davidic Empire) was divided into two nations; Israel (the Northern Kingdom) and Judah (the Southern Kingdom). By 722 BC, the wickedness of Ahab (and other wicked kings preceding him) had taken such a toll on the Northern Kingdom that it completely succumbed to the Assyrians as a vassal state. Israel was no more. One century later, In Josiah's time as king of the remaining Southern Kingdom of Judah, The Babylonians and Medes (The Neo-Babylonian Empire) were joining forces and rising in power against the Assyrians who exerted weak but overall control over Judah by its empirical influence. Before the end of Josiah's reign, the great city of Nineveh would fall to this Babylonian empire. Egypt's Pharaoh Neco II would soon invade during the latter part of Josiah's reign and cut a wide passage through Judah to aid the Assyrian empire against the Babylonians. The world was fast closing in on a God-forsaken Judah, the only remnant of the once great kingdom of Israel.

It is no innocent coincidence that Judah had fallen away from God. Abominations were everywhere and the people had not heard the Word of God, the God of David, in generations. The nation openly celebrated homosexuality and human sacrifice, not coincidentally the two gravest challenges facing our nation today. It had elevated pagan religions and rituals to a level that penetrated every "norm" of society. The path to destruction had been slowly yet relentlessly paved, and the people had long forgotten any fear of judgment from God. It is no wonder then that Judah in Josiah's day was one of the most immoral nations in the world. The seeds of the moral, political, and economic demise of Judah had been planted two centuries before. Judah, all that was left of the old Davidic Israel, was fading fast.

Stepping out of our time machine for a minute, let's see if we can draw a few comparisons to our own generation. It would seem a great parallel in history that few Americans in our day understand the ominous peril we face. We don't know God. Without His light we cannot see the destruction around us. Day after day, we tell ourselves we are in a great "recovery." But we are, in reality, whistling in the dark. We manipulate numbers, information, and even each other to maintain this great untruth. We print our currency into oblivion while our entire economy operates on how much debt we owe, not how much we produce. The security of the nation from external pressures, whether economical, ideological, or geopolitical, is laid bare by a paralyzed "morality" that can find no wrong in anything. There is no unified transcendent love for God or country. No binding holds the nation together.

We are a nation of individuals pretending to be united by a hyphen. But we cannot maintain the façade forever. Our enemies, envious of the many blessings from God we still hold, are licking their chops and sharpening their knives. Yet, lacking any national identity of our own anymore, we strive to be more like them every day. The outside world keeps moving toward a very dark day without America as the "beacon on a hill."

Our manifesto is to remind our nation of the God that binds us together while we march our way to that beacon, relight it, and guard it for the entire world to see.

Back into our time machine, we can see that the days of Josiah evolved from a series of bad leaders corrupting the nation for their own short-term political gains. In this case Manasseh, Josiah's extremely wicked grandfather and predecessor, brought the nation into wickedness to shore up his personal political power. Up to that time, the Southern Kingdom of Judea was itself a beacon to the nations, ever since the Northern Kingdom had been erased from the planet. But rather than stand with God as a light to the world, Manasseh took it upon himself to relieve the Southern Kingdom of its God-given uniqueness.

Perhaps he reasoned he could appease Assyria, the Babylonians, and the Medes if Judah looked more like its enemies than like Israel. He was a huge proponent of becoming one in thought with the other nations of the world, including the enemies of Israel. Manasseh adopted the neighboring nations' pagan religions, including human sacrifice. Incredibly, the tragic lesson of the fall of the Northern Kingdom had flown right over Manasseh's head. He imported abominations and perversion into his kingdom in the name of international and global unity. He abandoned the high ground God had assigned for Judah and adopted a high view of "globalism" over what God intended for the remnant of Israel. Because of its continuing outright defiance, God gave Judah over to its desires and, eventually, into the hands of its enemies.

The king who succeeded Manasseh, his son Amon, was well on his way to topping his father in iniquity when, two years into his reign, his own servants assassinated him. Such was the lowly state of the nation that brought eight-year-old Josiah to the throne. But as Josiah matured, he became sorely grieved by the wickedness permeating his kingdom. He reacted differently than his immediate ancestors. Josiah chose to stand, and by doing so, broke the cycle of evil.

On paper, this kid had no chance. But this boy-king grew to devote his entire heart, mind and soul, as well as his nation, to the one true God. Josiah's main obstacle was that the nation was profiting politically, albeit temporarily, by the weakness of Assyria and the lack of a viable threat from the still nascent Babylonian-Median empire. Everything was going so well outwardly that wickedness prevailed; there was no inward or outward pressure for the people to change their ways. But destruction was on the horizon, for such wickedness steadily rots *within*, crippling a nation *internally* until it cannot prevail against its *external* enemies.

Josiah was not the only godly man remaining in his kingdom. Biblical scholars tend to agree that a cadre of moral men and women must have tutored the young king. In thought and action, he was not his father's son. The scholars may be right, for he certainly did not inherit his repentant traits from his father or grandfather. One certain conclusion we can draw is this: the importance of offering godly advice to our leaders cannot be overstated.

Later, the Bible records a momentous occasion that changed the course of history for Judah under Josiah's watch. A particular archeological find, that under any other king might have simply been discarded, became a treasure that saved a nation, at least for a while. The miraculous occurrences from this point on in the biblical account starting in 2 Kings 22 were only possible because of one pivotal action: the singular response of Josiah. Upon his reaction alone, all else is built. We should remember this when we believe we are impotent against the unbeliever's onslaught. It is not what happens to us, but our *response,* that makes all the difference.

One of the saddest tragedies of Josiah's day was that the temple had fallen into terrible disrepair, a clear indication that the nation had abandoned God for a very long time. It was so bad, in fact, that pagan altars had been set up in the temple itself. Now remember, this is the temple Solomon had built in all its splendid glory. How far away the nation had slipped! By trying to mimic the world rather than cleave to God, the nation had lost its soul, its way, and its divine place on the world stage. Worse, the nation had blinded itself to its own pending demise. Though Judah was godless, outwardly it appeared to be prospering.

But such an outward façade cannot long deceive those inside the government who must lead the nation on the world stage. As Josiah matured on his throne, he became incensed by the daily human sacrifices, the pagan mumbo jumbo that led his people into stasis, ignorance, and blatant idolatry. Thus he began a slow but sure process of bringing the nation back to God. Eighteen years after Josiah inherited the throne, he commissioned a project to clear out and renovate the temple. He knew enough of the faith of his fathers to know that the temple, in past times, was the center of Davidic civilization. The temple was a reminder to the people of God's covenant with David, though no one quite remembered what that covenant was. The temple had been the House of God in what was left of Israel, and a reminder of the nation's former greatness, which had peaked during the reign of Solomon. Josiah set out to take a stand, reverse the advance of endless abominations, and restore his nation from the center out.

## "I Have Found The Book Of The Law In The House Of The Lord!"

These wondrous words from 2 Kings 22:8 resonate up from the musty, cobwebbed corridors of history right into the heart of every Christian living today.

While performing an accounting and cleanup of the temple, Hilkiah the high priest had found a long forgotten artifact deep within the temple. He gave it to Shaphan, the scribe, who read it to Josiah. What happened next was nothing less than a supernatural and godly reaction to the sudden revelation of truth. A searing light was now juxtaposed brightly against Judah's wickedness and the king was forced to decision point. Josiah had really only two options because the truth lay plainly for all to see. The nation could no longer continue to lie to itself and call its wickedness good. From now on, it would have to call its wickedness, wickedness.

Its only choice was either to repent or continue in wickedness, laying itself naked in its evil.

It is no wonder then that, once the book of the law was revealed, Josiah did not respond in joyful tears of thanksgiving. Upon hearing the Word of God firsthand and witnessing the stark contrast of wickedness around him, Josiah tore his clothes in deep mourning and despair. With a thunderclap, the Word of God had shattered the scales from his eyes. Visible now was the filth the entire nation had been wallowing in, exposed for all to see, no longer resembling the silken gold they had collectively deemed that filth to be.

Now, with a nation in mourning, Josiah consulted the prophets to discern God's instruction. Chief on their minds was the great pending destruction from God, provoked by the hardened heart of the nation. Josiah ordered the Word proclaimed to all the people of the land. On the very grounds of the dilapidated temple and in front of all the people, Josiah made a covenant with the Lord. With all of his heart and soul he swore to uphold the commandments and testimonies of the law they had re-discovered. And lo and behold, all the people swore the same. Whether or not the people truly meant their pledge is another story. Nevertheless, as commanded by God, Josiah set out to clean house and administer justice to those who had encouraged, peddled and profited from the wickedness that had destroyed his nation.

Scripture documents Josiah's complete dedication to God and his consistent efforts to counter enormous public opposition in order to bring about such abrupt change. In short, *he led his nation*; he did not follow its evil practices. He even destroyed the ritual booths providing both male and female cult prostitution "services" that had been set up near the temple. You can imagine the popularity of that move! Many scholars note that, in that day, heterosexual, bisexual and homosexual cult prostitution were all prevalent. Although the assassination of his predecessor was never far from his mind, Josiah still did not hesitate to rid the nation of such practices.

> *[The methods Josiah employed are an important study that is beyond the scope of this book. It is important to note that, under the Old Testament covenants, national leaders were many times commanded by God to kill His enemies. We are not under that covenant system today. We have to remember that the Messiah had not yet come, and the Holy Spirit had not yet been poured out to all those who believed. Rather, these events occur in the last days of the old covenant and in the last throes of Israel's struggle with God. But when the time was right, God would do as he promised and send a savior who would establish a new covenant. In our day of grace and mercy, God does not command us to kill anyone. Instead, He awaits our turning to Him. He has now opened the gates of Heaven to all who accept*

*His Son, not just to the biblical nation of Israel. In Josiah's time, however, God was honoring the specific covenants He had made with his people. There were inescapable earthly consequences if Israel broke its covenant with God.]*

Josiah burned, destroyed and otherwise obliterated the instruments of wickedness. He showed no mercy to those who had wantonly led the nation to destruction, and who had usually profited heavily. Scripture is not exactly specific on the issue but most biblical scholars infer that Josiah executed the pagan priests in the temple. This is certainly plausible. In Josiah's day, the God of Israel carried out immediate action through His people against its enemies.

[*Can you imagine the outcry if certain infrastructure supporting homosexuality and child sacrifice in our country today were suddenly decreed to be unacceptable, even if accomplished free of violence by a penitent nation?]*

The people in Josiah's day were shocked into action by the blinding contrast to their sin, exposed by the newly discovered book of the law. Led by a penitent leader, the nation pledged to turn back to God. This required heart action, not just empty words. Such was the radical action taken by Josiah in his day and such was the dedication to God and the strong leadership Josiah exercised over his wayward nation. Josiah's actions, by today's standards, may seem extremely harsh. That is because of our tendency is to mix historical context with today's context. So before we continue, lets get the context right.

**A Different Time, A Different Covenant**

Unbelievers have, in the past, attempted to misrepresent the covenantal differences between the New and Old Testaments, hoping to thrust into confusion and obscurity the enormously pivotal importance of Christ. By this they hope to demonstrate that the Bible is completely inconsistent. They deceitfully exploit the so-called "bloody" history of the Old Testament while completely ignoring the precious blood of the New Testament. Their hope is that those who are listening are completely ignorant of scripture.

So it bears repeating that the Holy Spirit had not yet been poured out upon the Earth; this would happen centuries later on the Day of Pentecost as foretold by the prophets Isaiah, Ezekiel, and Joel, among others. In the New Testament (under a new covenant with God's people) Jesus promised the Father would send the Holy Spirit in fulfillment of the scriptures (Isaiah 44:3, Ezekiel 39:29, Joel 2:28, Acts 2:17-21, John 14:16, 26, 15:26, 16:7). Please study these passages so that those who would pervert God's Word may not lead you astray. Josiah did not enjoy the incredible gift of the Holy Spirit you and I have today, for the Spirit had not yet been poured out among us.

What Josiah did was right in God's eyes, in his day, under God's applicable covenant. To properly draw a parallel to today, the lesson is taken not from Josiah's specific actions, but from his faithful and courageous decision to lead the nation into repentance under God. Remembered in the proper biblical context, the lesson we draw from Josiah is crucial to taking our stand in the 21st century.

In Josiah's day, God would instead specifically anoint individual prophets with the Holy Spirit as He saw fit. Sometimes leaders voluntarily consulted these prophets, and at other times they were sent by God to announce His Word. An excellent example is the prophetess Hulduh. Josiah consulted this prophetess, who delivered a bittersweet message to him. God would indeed carry out the wrath irreversibly brought on by Judah's years of truly evil deeds. There was no salvation or rescue because the wages of sin is death and there was, as yet, no Savior. The Son of God, the anointed advocate, had yet to bear the sins of the people in such a way as to save the world, much less Judah. Those who loved God would be saved by Christ's work on the cross in time, but the nation of Judah, its heart hardened beyond permanent repair, could not be saved.

Graciously, though, God honored Josiah's tender heart, promising the king he would enjoy the fruits of his work for the Lord and experience peace throughout his lifetime. Josiah was spared from seeing the day when his nation was taken into captivity. While he lived, God blessed the nation. However, we should all note that God's ultimate judgment was final. Even so, this did not stop or even discourage Josiah from carrying out his promise to do everything possible to revive his nation toward God.

Pray that, like Josiah, we will be able to serve the Lord to the best of our ability and let God decide the outcome.

## Under A New Covenant

We have reason to believe our outcome will be quite different. We live in a different time and under a new covenant. For us, the Holy Spirit leads, making a way where currently none exists. But certainly, if godly Americans dedicate the heart and soul of their nation to Him as Josiah did in his time, God *will cleanse our nation from wickedness*. This is a promised certainty. Once accomplished, will it last? That is a relative question since we know from Revelation and from the prophets that ultimately heaven and earth will pass away, to be replaced by a new heaven and earth. So how long a revived nation lasts is irrelevant. What is relevant, always, is our obedience to God.

True believers must no longer sit on their hands as destruction and the real threat of abandonment by God draws near. But we hold no delusions. As we take our stand, there will be some unhappy people who refuse to accept

Christ, even as today they continue to corrupt the foundation of our nation. Persistent in their sin, even when surrounded by the celebration of the Gospel, they will feel some isolation and discomfort. As God once again becomes undeniably visible and stands in stark contrast to their wickedness, the twin spotlights of truth and recognition of the need for repentance will be restored. For remember that the unbeliever's first mission is to abolish shame. But the day is coming when, in the light of God's love, they will be ostracized if they choose to continue down the road of destruction.

Every Christian in the United States today can identify with that sense of isolation. Isolation of the Christian has been the unbelievers' goal, which allows them to carry out their wickedness unhindered. Conversely, we do not want unbelievers to be isolated; they will, however, isolate themselves as some continue to stand in defiance while a majority of Americans revive their original commitment to God and country.

Many hearts will soften to the point of salvation, but as in the days of Josiah, some will not. Those who will not allow the light of truth into their hearts will continue to mock, attack, and attempt to silence us.

If you would, take a short moment and read Psalm 80. Lets us pray together and often that the Lord would restore us, though our enemies laugh at us (Psalm 80:6).

In the next chapter, we will come to understand God's role in the hardened heart. We can do that by walking right into the very next psalm – Psalm 81. We all tend to think one-dimensionally at times. But for every action we take individually, like ripples in a pond, many others are affected. Moreover, God is active in our lives. Our individual actions are only a part of the story. God, our Father in heaven, is also intricately involved with man. In a similar manner, there are earthly consequences to an unbeliever's actions. The consequences of sin tend to act more like a riptide than ripples in a pond. Christians have been caught up in that riptide, but we now recognize that taking a consistent stand for Christ against that current is the only way to eventually calm the waters.

## Chapter Eight

# ...And God Gave Them Over

It is our *response* to God that either hardens our heart or brings us to salvation.

Scripture is replete with examples of God literally giving sinners over to their propensity to sin. Yet we are also told that God's grace is still available to every sinner alive. Not only is this a point of contention among unbelievers, but many Christians also struggle with this apparent biblical inconsistency. However, since the Bible also tells us that God is immutable, unchanging, and entirely consistent, we know that this only *appears* to be an inconsistency. It serves as a red flag that a deeper study of God and His Word is needed.

We must endeavor to understand the underlying basis for God "giving sinners over" to their iniquity – an apparent abandonment, if not downright betrayal, by a God who has promised salvation. In such a study, we begin to eat real meat, putting away the baby bottle. And even that is just the beginning. For we will spend all eternity with Him, in awe each day, as we forever learn more about Him. For we will no longer have to rely on His written Word, inspired by Him and recorded by man, seeing Him through a glass darkly. We will see Him face-to-face, in His blinding light, learning from His own mouth as we marvel at the God of the universe for all eternity.

But for now, we are to set about studying His Word to mine the gold that is nestled within. The question before us is this: What does it mean when God gives someone over to sin? As we take our stand, we will need to be well grounded in our faith, for this question, whether presented honestly or as a sinner's challenge, must be answered truthfully with its full meaning packed into our response. The answer represents the foundational core of God's relationship with man, whom He created in His own image. If a sinner asks this question of you, and is willing to listen, you will expose him to a truth so astounding that he will never be the same whatever direction he takes when he leaves you. Such is the power of the Holy Spirit that dwells within us.

**There Comes A Time...**

If we sin long enough with no forthcoming contrition, we have no claim even to God's grace. Remember that grace is freely given even though we have no right to it. This is an amazing gift. Yet there comes a time, if sin continues, where God simply withdraws his restraint and "delivers" the sinner to his own desires.

The same is true with nations. That is because there comes a time, known only to God, when sin has been perfected and rejection of God's grace is complete. In this situation, as we have mentioned before, sin and God cannot occupy the same space. Jesus was both God and Man and dwelt among us (John 1:14). But Jesus was without sin. Note that *God* makes the initial outreach, crossing the boundary into enemy territory to save us from sin. *He calls us first.* Then there is a struggle until either the sinner surrenders his will to God or settles into lifelong defiance. Depending on the person, that struggle can last a few minutes or endure for decades. Chances are that someone with whom you have shared the Gospel is already wrestling with God, having already heard God's calling. You and I, powered by the Holy Spirit, are instruments in God's rescue attempt for such a person.

Consider this question: if a person has just jumped overboard into the freezing waters and knows he is about to drown, why would he not reach for the lifesaver? Or if your own children know their next step is living and begging on the street, with no warmth, no money, no food, why would they vow never to return to hearth and home?

Our question is based on a false premise. It assumes that one's decision and its consequences occur instantaneously. The heart does not harden abruptly, but slowly, incrementally. By the time we realize we are separated from our God (like the drowning man or the wayward child), we have already gone a long way down a very slippery slope. Satan brings us along one step at a time. With each footfall away from Christ, it becomes more difficult to extricate ourselves from this diabolical progression.

**Move The Line**

If you have ever played "move the line" with your small child, you know what I mean. "Jeffery, don't take another step towards the stove or Daddy will be mad." The child takes the dare, and the step. "Jeffery, that's enough. Daddy is serious now. Don't you dare take another step." The child takes another step because he is enjoying his current power over Daddy, though, at that age, he is not quite aware of this reason for his disobedience. Jeffery is enjoying a newfound independence he doesn't fully understand.

This is Jeffery's intrinsic, inborn sinful nature giving him the illusion of earthly pleasure, his first taste of pure, unadulterated power. It's a seemingly happy place. He wants more of it, so much so that he is willing to risk discipline. He has no inkling of the consequences. Despite the warnings, the discipline seems long in coming. For now, the power he holds is immediate and intoxicating. The analogy, however, is not complete because at some point, Daddy will physically intervene because the child is too young to exercise free will.

But fast-forward to college years. Daddy will have to let Jeffery make his own mistakes, perhaps fatally, if he continues his willful disobedience. There comes a point when Daddy has to let Jeffery exercise his own free will, whatever the consequences. We know of parents who have had to let willfully disobedient teens run away, or when coming of age, even kick them out of the house because the entire household is at risk if they stay. I'm not advocating this; I'm just saying that it happens. A heart hardens in gradual stages, and at some point, if not checked, the damage becomes irreversible. Even worse, it progresses, not only to total separation, but to outright war against God.

**A Fatal Progression**

In order to understand the progression of the hardened heart against God's Word, the colossal damage it brings, and God's response to it, we need look no further than the Bible itself.

Scripture clearly documents this, most notably in Romans 1:18-32 and Psalm 81. These passages trace a sad progression, demonstrating how a loving God must deliver one of His own creation over to evil. It is a stunning account and a reminder that sin brings consequences and that ultimate sin leads to ultimate consequences.

Let us first examine Romans 1:18 and following verses. Feel free to use your own reputable translation alongside this study. For instance, an older person like myself might prefer something like the King James Version, or a younger person might prefer something along the lines of The Living Bible. I chose the NASB because I believe it represents one of the best compromises between strict Greek grammatical structure and everyday modern English language equivalents to convey the closest possible interpretation of the original Greek text of the New Testament.

*Romans 1:18-32*
*The Progression of the Hardened Heart*

*"18 For the wrath of God is revealed from heaven against all ungodliness and unrighteousness of men who suppress the truth in unrighteousness,*
*19 because that which is known about God is evident within them; for God made it evident to them.*
*20 For since the creation of the world His invisible attributes, His eternal power and divine nature, have been clearly seen, being understood through what has been made, so that they are without excuse.*
*21 For even though they knew God, they did not honor Him as God or give thanks, but they became futile in their speculations, and their foolish heart was darkened.*
*22 Professing to be wise, they became fools,*
*23 and exchanged the glory of the incorruptible God for an image in the form of corruptible*

man and of birds and four-footed animals and crawling creatures.

24 Therefore God gave them over in the lusts of their hearts to impurity, so that their bodies would be dishonored among them.

25 For they exchanged the truth of God for a lie, and worshiped and served the creature rather than the Creator, who is blessed forever. Amen.

26 For this reason God gave them over to degrading passions; for their women exchanged the natural function for that which is unnatural,

27 and in the same way also the men abandoned the natural function of the woman and burned in their desire toward one another, men with men committing indecent acts and receiving in their own persons the due penalty of their error.

28 And just as they did not see fit to acknowledge God any longer, God gave them over to a depraved mind, to do those things which are not proper,

> 29 *being filled with all unrighteousness, wickedness, greed, evil; full of envy, murder, strife, deceit, malice; they are gossips,*
>
> 30 *slanderers, haters of God, insolent, arrogant, boastful, inventors of evil, disobedient to parents,*
>
> 31 *without understanding, untrustworthy, unloving, unmerciful;*
>
> 32 *and although they know the ordinance of God, that those who practice such things are worthy of death, they not only do the same, but also give hearty approval to those who practice them."*

The hardening of the heart begins with the mind turning from God, leading almost immediately toward impurity and dishonor of the body. This progresses quickly into all sorts of depravity down a very slippery slope. Worst of all, it ends in total defiance of God to the point that one actually instructs and exhorts others to openly defy God and take up battle against Him.

This is how it starts:

**Suppressing The Truth**

*"1:18 For the wrath of God is revealed from Heaven against all ungodliness and unrighteousness of men who suppress the truth in unrighteousness."*

In order to sin and escape condemnation from his fellow man, the unbeliever must suppress the truth. And if we are going to pass laws that allow us to sin, the truth must be obscured on a national scale. It follows that Christians who represent the God of truth must be marginalized in order for a nation to become unrighteous in God's eyes. If an unbeliever rejects God, he must continuously attempt to obliterate the presence of the Holy Spirit who lights the way to truth to all who seek it. The Holy Spirit will always be evident to those who have accepted Christ and know God's Word. The unbeliever's task is to sow doubt into the heart of the believer while discouraging all others from seeking the truth that God has placed all around them. It's a very dangerous smoke and mirrors act. Once he purposely discards the truth, the unbeliever is on the road to ruin because he must never again allow truth to raise its head; soon, anything goes.

As long as the Holy Spirit is present in believers who stand on God's truth, the unbeliever can never rest. He must continually "double down" on his efforts to deceive. His sin takes him farther than he ever meant to go. Repentance is the only way out, but repentance becomes harder with each subsequent step he takes away from the truth. Each step stores up God's wrath.

As we begin to turn away from God, we do store up His wrath. Remember this is the wrath against sin, which cannot coexist with God. This wrath was satisfied on the cross and thus that propitiation (Christ's atonement on the cross) is available to every believer. However, no one gets a pass from this wrath until he reconciles with God, changes his ways (repents), and is then covered by God's grace through Christ's death and resurrection.

Beware the "Christian" who does not ever seek forgiveness; he is revealed to never have given his life to God. For a Christian to long remain in a state of sin with God is antithetical to Christianity. He may call himself a Christian. Many do. But since Christianity is defined by a personal relationship with the one true living God, through Jesus Christ, God knows those who are truly His.

## They Have No Excuse

> *"1:19 Because that which is known about God is evident within them; for God made it evident to them.*

*1:20 For since the creation of the world His invisible attributes, His eternal power and divine nature, have been clearly seen, being understood through what has been made, so that they are without excuse."*

The unbeliever knows what he is doing as he willfully turns away from God. And he has no excuse because God has made His presence known simply by the external revelation of creation all around us, as well as the self-evidence of God in our hearts.

There is no explaining our universe apart from God. Many have tried, but in the end there is no other answer for a causal nature of the universe.

As we will see, the end result of turning away from God eventually leads to rejecting Him completely. It is going to be difficult, but certainly not impossible, for the unbeliever to reverse the process he has started. He would have to admit his error, readmit the truth into his heart, and allow God to heal it.

The conflict roiling inside unbelievers persuades them that they would be very happy if the "truth carriers" would simply disappear. If we did not have the capacity to determine truth, we could not be held responsible for sin in the first place. The unbeliever yearns for a place where he is completely free to sin and claim ignorance or helplessness. This is the Tropical Island of Irresponsibility where the unbeliever hopes to set up residence. That island does not exist.

But the blinding light that irritates them and prevents them from settling into sin unmolested by the truth is the very light that can save them if they let it. Despite their efforts to suppress that light, it will never be extinguished until God snatches all living Christians up in the air in the rapture to come. Woe shall betide the unbeliever in that day. Prior to that day, can this person be saved? Yes, certainly. There is still a chance. It is just more difficult for the person who rejects the knowledge of God's existence, which is evident in his own heart and all around him.

**A Deadly Exchange**

> *"1:21 For even though they knew God, they did not honor Him as God or give thanks, but they became futile in their speculations, and their foolish heart was darkened.*
>
> *1:22 Professing to be wise, they became fools,*
>
> *1:23 and exchanged the glory of the incorruptible God for an image in the form of corruptible man and of birds and four-footed animals and crawling creatures."*

Now the inevitable rationalization begins. But note that an exchange occurs here. You cannot walk away from God and keep Him. God created us and we belong to Him. If we leave him, however, we are still not our own; we belong to Satan, the Father of All Lies and the Prince of This Age. When we put ourselves in God's place, we make ourselves idols by default. We then profess to have the wisdom of our own making rather than that of the incorruptible God. As we profess to be wise, we become fools because there is no wisdom apart from God. After exchanging His incorruptible form for our own corruption, our speculations now become foolish and our hearts subsequently darken.

Back there in the dust, somewhere, is God. We have rejected Him and left Him behind. In such a circumstance, what can God's response be?

## So Be It

God could only give them over to the lusts of their hearts. That's where they wanted to go, and to that place he let them land.

*"1:24 Therefore God gave them over in the lusts of their hearts to impurity, so that their bodies would be dishonored among them.*

*1:25 For they exchanged the truth of God for a lie and worshiped and served the creature rather than the Creator, who is blessed forever. Amen."*

They now pursue impurity with a vengeance. With nothing to stop them, the earthly consequences of sin sink into their souls and dishonor enters their bodies. Even though they claim to be the author of their own destinies, they don't even respect the sacredness that remains of their own corruptible body, the very vessel in which they inhabit this earth.

Now we are progressing with ever increasing swiftness toward a thoroughly hardened heart. God has removed His restraint and will allow their sin to run to its inevitable conclusion. This is the first giving over. Look how far this unbeliever has gone. He has refused to acknowledge the truth of God within him. He has willfully and repeatedly turned away from God, going his own natural in-born way (in truth, the way of Satan). Because he wants nothing to do with God, God can no longer hold him close and restrain him.

The "Amen" at the end is Paul simply saying, "so be it." He wants the Romans to know that these consequences do not delight him, but rather, are the inevitable consequences of turning away from God. In today's language, instead of "Amen," Paul might say "It is what it is."

You might think our sinner could go no further astray, but you would be wrong. This is only the beginning.

## Abandonment Of Natural Function

*"1:26 For this reason God gave them over to degrading passions; for their women exchanged the natural function for that which is unnatural,*

*1:27 and in the same way also the men abandoned the natural function of the woman and burned in their desire toward one another, men with men committing indecent acts and receiving in their own persons the due penalty of their error."*

Paul is speaking directly and unmistakably about homosexuality here. Why now at this point in the epistle? As Paul has said, turning the mind away from God leads immediately to bodily impurity, which is now infected by the corruption of the mind. Since we are bodily human beings, when there is no right or wrong for our mind, there can be no right or wrong for our bodies either.

Despite modern homosexual apologetics, homosexuality is SOUNDLY condemned in scripture (Genesis 19; Leviticus 18:22; 1 Corinthians 6:9-11; Galatians 5:19-21; Ephesians 5:3-5; 1 Timothy 1:9-10; Jude 7, and of course, Romans 1). Paul is showing the progression of sin toward its most stark and costly conclusions. He considered homosexuality to be a shocking consequence of lust descending into depravity by a corrupt mind and body. His intent is to indelibly mark such sin as a perilous milestone that can be reached once God begins to give one over to his sin. He seems to say that there is no end to the depravity once one starts down that road. For corruption of the mind is inextricably connected to corruption of the body.

This passage is solid evidence that the early church certainly was aware of the practice and did indeed view it as a grave sin. It was prevalent in that time and stood in contrast to a believer's living and active faith in God, just as it does today.

Some have written that Paul was not talking about homosexuality because it didn't exist in his day. It was unfamiliar to him, they claim. Interestingly, others on the same side (the wrong side of the cross) proclaim that homosexuality has always been around as a natural proclivity, genetic or otherwise. They can't have it both ways. To say that Paul was not familiar with homosexuality in his day and did not address it is to disregard known history, both external to the Bible and from primary evidence offered in the Bible.

Why does Paul mention women first in the homosexuality passage? Many scholars believe it is not because they introduced this sin, (and by inference led men to do it) but rather to show the length of depravity that EVEN women participated. In New Testament times women, by culture if not by scripture, were subservient to the husband in the spiritual matters of the household. The husband, as it was with Adam, was (and still is) responsible for spiritual leadership of the family. That even women were practicing homosexuality, bypassing any male leadership, proves Paul's concern about the depth of the depravity and amplifies the emphasis Paul placed on it.

Although this discourse uses homosexuality as an extreme example of the consequences that await one who exchanges the truth of God for a lie, the broader context includes *any sin* stemming from a propensity toward impurity. Paul eloquently illustrates the process of God reluctantly giving sinners over until they are finally and totally lost, even to the point of actually taking up battle against Him. That is the ultimate hardened heart.

## The Slippery Slide Of Satan's Slope

Let's step back for a moment and see how far we have come. Unbelievers have now moved beyond suppressing the truth to entertaining speculation outside of God, thus becoming foolish. This propensity for foolishness then leads them into outright lust for impurity, landing them straight into a pit of degrading passion. Each time it worsens, and they inch closer to becoming irreversible disciples of Satan. They will erroneously believe and proclaim that they are free, unencumbered by "superstition" and are much more intelligent than any "fool" who would submit himself to a God that "does not exist." Truly, the only freedom they have is to pace back and forth within their ever-shrinking cage. We can't stop here long because they are whooshing past us still further into depravity.

> *"1:28 And just as they did not see fit to acknowledge God any longer, God gave them over to a depraved mind, to do those things which are not proper"*

Now, moving down the staircase of degrading passions, the sinner quickly succumbs to a completely *depraved mind* filled with all kinds of evil, none of them proper. This progression is unavoidable, a natural path for those choosing to turn from God. Note that all of the previous actions have finally led the sinner to *no longer acknowledge God*. The ties have been cut, the bonds released, and the boundaries erased. The verse makes it clear that *because they acknowledged God no longer,* He gave them over to a depraved mind. But just what is the character of a depraved mind? We continue in Romans 1.

## No Vestige Of God Remaining

There is still one more level to descend, so note that their betrayal of the Creator, even at this stage, is not yet fully complete. Sadly, there is still an even worse "giving over," precipitated of course by the previous steps on this downward path to hell. These people, empty of any goodness, have no vestige of God left in them.

> *"1:29 being filled with all unrighteousness, wickedness, greed, evil; full of envy, murder, strife, deceit, malice; they are gossips,*

*1:30 slanderers, haters of God, insolent, arrogant, boastful, inventors of evil, disobedient to parents,*

*1:31 without understanding, untrustworthy, unloving, unmerciful"*

They are out there. Some are in power in Washington, D.C., and some live right around the corner. Oh, they will claim goodness, enlightenment, spirituality, and, of course, humility. But, in fact, their actions and their own words betray them. We meet people who will not hold a civil conversation with us if we disagree with them in any way. Quickly turning to ad homonym attacks to shut you down, they cannot deal with any facts you present, because the truth is foreign to them.

## Certified Instructors Of Evil

*"1:32 and although they know the ordinance of God, that those who practice such things are worthy of death, they not only do the same, but also give hearty approval to those who practice them."*

Now they have reached the bottom of the downward progression to the ultimate hardened heart. These people *know* that they oppose God (no more excuses of ignorance) yet take it a step further. *They do it anyway.* Think about that for a moment. They know God's Word; they heard what God says about the consequences of their actions. They freely acknowledge that they are "God haters." But it gets even worse. They actually approve, encourage, and give their hearty consent to all those who do the same. Although scripture does not specifically say that they teach (disciple) others in evil, the inference is quite clear by their "hearty approval."

These people are God's greatest enemies on Earth. They have bunkered their hearts within a ton of concrete where God is not allowed.

**From Stubborn Hearts To Depraved Hearts**

So why does God give people over to their sin? Psalm 81 gives us a clear picture of how these people start down this path and why they end up here.

*"81:11 "But my people would not listen to me; Israel would not submit to me.*

*81:12 So I gave them over to their stubborn hearts to follow their own devices."*

His people, "the sheep of his pasture" (Psalm 100:3), would not listen, would not submit. He created us; therefore we belong to Him. In contrast, those whom God has given over began their journey by closing their ears to Him, unwilling to listen to or submit to Him. From there it is a short step toward suppressing the truth. Without that foundational truth they began to form their own foolish speculations, causing their hearts to become foolish and darkened. Further, they did not give glory to God. Now they are given over to degrading passions with and against one another. Without a need to retain any knowledge of God, down they descend into depravity. Finally, not stopping there, they encourage others to do the same. No wonder the Christian is under such ferocious attack by these unbelievers. The Christian is well aware of the danger they pose.

There is, however, a catch. It is not for us to give them over. That is God's domain. So if the Holy Spirit leads you to someone, regardless of his assumed status with God, you MUST witness to him. This job is not for the weak in spirit; but again, if God leads, you must go. Skipping over "bad people" is not the point of this chapter or this book. The goal is to be able to recognize that some people have hardened their hearts. We all have to understand what that means, how they got there, and that they are at some stage of being given over. Remember that they are not the enemy; they are *deceived* by the enemy. Bless the hardened heart to which God has sent a witness! One day, it might be you He sends. But at least now you know the path upon which every unbeliever treads. You know why some have been given over and that your task is urgent.

A warning here is warranted. Be on guard! If *you* want to avoid any chance of being given over, spend a good amount of time in Psalm 19. The psalmist here shows a reverse progression of the one presented in the last half of Romans 1. Meditate on Psalm 19 often and you will always know where you stand.

# Chapter Nine

# Put On The Full Armor Of God

We are to take up the full armor, resist, and do everything we can to *stand firm.* So now it is time to get dressed for battle.

> *"6:11 Put on the full armor of God, so that you will be able to stand firm against the schemes of the devil.*
>
> *6:12 For our struggle is not against flesh and blood, but against the rulers, against the powers, against the world forces of this darkness, against the spiritual forces of wickedness in the heavenly places.*

*6:13 Therefore, take up the full armor of God, so that you will be able to resist in the evil day, and having done everything, to stand firm."*

Many Christians have trouble incorporating any kind of spiritual warfare or martial sense into their walk with Christ. They suffer from too many soft sermons, too many admonitions to be non-confrontational. These admonitions are issued from those who easily claim the "comfortable" aspects of their faith but cringe when duty calls. Yes, confrontation is uncomfortable. But look around. The sandbags are piling up right in front of you. Precious ground has been given over through our misguided efforts to remain comfortable. It is a treasonous tradeoff.

"Beloved, I do not want you to be ignorant" (as Paul would say), so that you know with absolute certainty that scripture calls every Christian to be active in spiritual warfare. As we have seen and learned by our own experience, we are under attack by those who willfully practice evil. Even so, we spiritual warriors have been armed both defensively and offensively by Christ to *stand firm*.

The Holy Spirit dwells within us and guides us all the way, but only if we listen and obey. If we close our spiritual ears, we will take up our own foolish speculations and, professing to be wise, we shall become fools in short order. To be brutally frank, that is what got us into a mess in the first place.

## A New Manifesto

But those days are over. It's a new day. All across the nation, we will be working together to put the Gospel of Jesus Christ back on the menu. We have our priorities. We will pray alone. We will pray together. We can talk about the latest American Idol, or we can talk about the difference Christ has made in our lives. We can talk about the latest Hollywood scandal, or we can talk about the scandal of sin that has been forever removed from our destiny. If they tell us they don't want to hear it, fine; we respect that. We've honored God and it's time to move on. But that doesn't mean that when we hear error we will not defend the Gospel. We will defend it every time. We won't let error hang in the air because when error goes unchallenged, our silence makes us culpable. An unbeliever can silence the claxon call for his own salvation, but the Christian must never remain silent about the truth of the Gospel.

You may feel very much embarrassed at first. That's normal. At this point many people would give advice that goes something like this: "But ask yourself, if you were standing before God with this person who was going to hell, would you be ashamed?" I think that is terrible advice. You don't control this person's salvation or where he spends eternity. Your only responsibility is to give him a message and offer correction if he is in error about the Gospel. If he wants to know more about Jesus, bring him into discipleship. If not, honor his choice and pray for him because his fate lies with Satan until he repents. By these actions, we remind the people of this country that the Holy Spirit is present among us. The path to salvation and certain hope in Christ, after two thousand years, is still open.

If you are nervous or ever frightened to speak up when you know you should, remember who you are. Remember that unbelievers are not nervous or frightened about sharing their beliefs. Remember that they count on your silence to continue on the path of destruction that is dragging your country right to the brink. Remember that the Holy Spirit is with you and will give you the words to say if you rely on Him. Remember the Cross of Jesus. You'll know what to do.

Don't try to grade yourself. Don't get into a silly argument or a debate about the veracity of the Bible. Just honestly tell the person what you believe, and that you have been convinced by the evidence and by your personal relationship with Jesus Christ. Tell him the truth, that you have committed your life to Christ and that you are positively persuaded that He is able to keep that which you have committed to Him against that day when He comes to take you home (2 Timothy 1:12). Let your life be your witness, for your example is there for all to see. Do this with love in your heart and *listen to him*. Hear him out, but be firm in your faith. That's all you can do, but the good news is *that's all God asks of you*. He does the rest. And the angels shall rejoice in the glory you have given God by your courageous *action*, powered by your faith through God's grace.

It is important to speak up as often as we can, not only for our nation but also for the lost. Having studied in a Baptist seminary, I can tell you that we Baptists have a strange phobia about Mack trucks. For some reason we hold a certain belief that the proverbial Mack truck is lurking around the corner of every conversation with an unbeliever. We fear that in the next minute a Mack truck will come out of nowhere and run the poor fellow down. Thus we never let a person go without sharing Christ when the opportunity arises. It's a good motivator, but I wouldn't live in fear of Mack trucks! Although I kid my fellow evangelicals about that mythical Mack truck, I am touched that their love for the lost demonstrates such a clear sense of urgency. It doesn't matter what denomination you belong to, if any. We all need to nurture that sense of urgency because Satan excels at dulling it in both the lost and the saved.

In spiritual warfare we are not to attack Satan. That battle belongs to the Lord who has already defeated him. We are only to claim, stand, and hold the territory God delivered in that victory. Speaking up is a key component in that responsibility. In our immediate context as American citizens, that means we stand on and hold to the original founding principles of our great nation, The United States of America. It was founded as a "beacon on a hill," where all are free from tyranny and persecution, acknowledging that God has granted man certain unalienable rights. These rights do not ebb and flow from man at the whim of man; rather, they are endowed upon man by our Creator.

We did not create a theocracy. We founded, by God's hand, a nation where truth and freedom reign supreme. Where truth reigns in ultimate freedom, so does the one true living God through His free gift of salvation. All beliefs, under the framework of our Constitution, are free from persecution in this land because the unfettered truth of the Gospel, when allowed to be heard unhindered, enters the heart of all those who seek and are able to hear the truth. Therefore we do not fear freedom of speech or the constitutional practice of any religion because honest men and women will always diligently strive to discern truth from fiction. In a fair forum, Christianity has nothing to fear from any religion or government. And no religion or legitimate government has anything to fear from Christianity.

Alas, we have voluntarily surrendered so many of those rights through spiritual inaction that rarely can a fair forum now be found. We are in a spiritual battle for the survival of our nation and, indeed, the very survival of that spiritual ground God so graciously gave us. As long as we held the ground God gave us, it was a fair fight, so to speak. This is why, as we noted in the beginning of this book, we seem to be fighting at a disadvantage. So much of the ground we were given to stand upon has already been surrendered. We are very near our own end zone.

If you like, you might look upon *Return of the Christian* as a half-time pep talk! By the power of the Holy Spirit, we can take back our territory. We can do all things through God who strengthens us (Philippians 4:13). But we are going to have to revert to the original playbook and stop worrying about how big those guys out there look. We need to stop listening to their "game talk." They're only human, after all.

We have no right to seize hold of Christ with one hand while surrendering that which He has entrusted to us in the other. The battle is His. We are His. This ground is ours to hold for Him until He comes to claim us. We are to boldly share the Gospel while protecting ourselves with the panoply of armor he has provided us against those who foolishly but diligently seek to destroy His very presence among us. The Gospel gains ground through the Holy Spirit. As it is shared and received, the Holy Spirit advances. Our job: stand and hold the ground that has been won through the power of the Holy Spirit. It's not easy, but this is not a new problem, as we note in Paul's first epistle to the Thessalonians:

> *"2:1 For you yourselves know, bretheren, that our coming to you was not in vain;*

*2:2 but after already suffering and being mistreated in Philippi, as you know, we had the boldness in our God to speak to you the Gospel of God, amid much opposition."*

When we stand, the world will oppose us. As you can see, though, we are in good company. If Paul was not spared difficulties, neither will we. But look what happened! God's Word does not return void, *ever*. After Paul had shared the Gospel amid much opposition in Thessalonica, he received glowing reports of the growth and boldness of that church.

*"1:6 You became imitators of us, and of our Lord, having received the Word in much tribulation with the joy of the Holy Sprit.*

*1:7 So that you became an example to all the believers in Macedonia and Achaia.*

*1:8 For the Word of the Lord has sounded forth from you not only in Macedonia and Achaia, but also in every place your faith toward God has gone forth, so that we have no need to say anything."*

This is why Paul could say, "Our coming to you was not in vain." If it were not for Paul's boldness in the face of opposition and tribulation, the Thessalonians would not have matured to share the Gospel even further into Macedonia and Achaia. Inexplicably, the Christian church seems to grow and even flourish under opposition. If that is the case, we are in for one heck of a growth spurt! This will surely come, but only if we put on the full armor of God and boldly speak the Gospel of God amid that opposition.

## One Nation, Under God

The armor defends us as well. Without it, we fall as easy prey to the "schemes" of unbelievers.

Some Christians in our own day even question the premise that our nation is and shall be one nation under God. They have for several decades allowed themselves to speculate as the world does, whether any nation should be under God. The main culprit seems to be the vast multitude of warm, breathy sermons emanating from under-heated churches. They steam up the windows of our faith. They cozy up our enclosure until we can no longer see the ever-growing cemetery just outside the fogged windowpanes.

One only has to look at Joshua and Matthew 28:19-20 to know that in both the old and new covenants God grants title to His own. But there is a condition. They must *possess it*. The admonishment in Matthew 28:19 is to "go and make disciples..." The predominant verb in the original Greek is the word "go": to *go into the land* and make disciples. You and I are commissioned to take possession of His territory, a place in which we do not yet dwell, and by sharing the Gospel, to make disciples there. If we follow that commission in our own country, citizens will vote much differently than they do today. There is no commission in scripture to surrender what God has already graciously given to us.

Joshua was commanded by God to go and take *possession* of the land God had already given to His people, a land they did not currently occupy. There was no Holy Spirit poured out upon the nations in Joshua's day. There was no Gospel of salvation in Jesus Christ. In that day, God commanded them to take physical possession. Now that the Holy Spirit is among us, we are to take *spiritual* possession.

A rancher knows that he may hold title to a section of land, but if he does not patrol it, *possess it*, squatters frequently settle in. By default the rancher eventually no longer *possesses* the land to which he holds title. He must go into the land and patrol it to maintain the boundaries and remove any squatters before they overtake the land by right of common possession. In this day of grace we are charged with that same spiritual responsibility.

By the way, if you are thinking of our nation's borders at this moment, you are beginning to understand the biblical scope of possessing, standing, and holding the territory for which you own title. You are also acknowledging the consequences of failing to do so. A border literally defines a nation. Only a government despotically desperate to hold onto power at any cost would trade its own borders for power. It is a temporary, senseless, and doomed death grasp for power that cannot long be sustained.

This also serves as an apt analogy to those "Christians" who adopt the same faulty measures to "maintain" their church at all costs. Their borders become undefined, their biblical boundaries blurred. The very souls of their churches are eventually corrupted from within until they are no different from the world that surrounds them.

To complete the analogy, a church that holds to the Gospel serves its divine purpose by giving glory to God, no matter its size. God always honors such a church. Our nation, if it adheres to its Constitution, will serve its divine purpose in the same way, allowing God-given freedom and equal opportunity to flow to every citizen while rendering to God His due glory. God always protects and honors a nation after His own heart.

**The Great Recession**

If you have taken a good look around lately, that God-given freedom to all mankind is fast disappearing from the nations of the world. Such is the divine uniqueness of the United States of America and its historic destiny as a beacon on a hill.

I mentioned earlier that the surrender of our spiritual title to God-given territory has occurred by recession. We have receded, with our Christ-given light, into our bunkers. In effect, many of us hold our light under a basket. Jesus directly admonishes us to avoid this apostasy in the Gospel of Luke:

*"11:33 No one, after lighting a lamp, puts it away in a cellar nor under a basket, but on the lampstand, so that those who enter may see the light."*

It bears repeating: we carry the light of Christ and no darkness can overcome it. The only way darkness advances is if light recedes.

How do we turn back the darkness?

**Stand On The WHOLE Gospel**

We do so first by recognizing our commission from God beginning with Matthew 28:19-20 which, in one form or another, permeates the entire Gospel.

Secondly, begin not from the place to which we have currently retreated. We must stand on the *whole* Gospel, and not upon the narrow end zone we have left. It has always been our commission to stand on the *whole* Gospel, which is unchanging. We cannot decide to take a stand on the Gospel and then simply defend what we have left. We stand on the *whole* Gospel or we lie down in defeat. The Gospel confronts a lost world by demonstrating the need to reconcile with the one true living God. So when, by the Holy Spirit, we confront unbelievers with the truth, we must rely on the *whole* truth. That is the Gospel.

In doing so, I think you can imagine the stark contrast confronting the unbeliever when we stand on the *entire continent of the Gospel* rather than upon the few islands we have yet to surrender. We reside in an info-crowded world where multiple new and old age concepts vie for acceptance. Nothing but the alarming comparison between the Gospel and the perilous path of our nation can possibly seize the unbeliever's attention and convey the true urgency of his situation.

To stand on the whole Gospel, for instance, avoids useless bickering in the semantics that remain to us as a result of the changes in language unbelievers have dictated over the last 40 years to disguise sin. You can't expose the truth if the language you speak is rigged to disguise it.

When Josiah found the Word of the Lord in the temple ruins, the entire nation was brought to sorrow and repentance because the Word they found was in its original form, unchanged from the day it was first written. It represented a stark contrast and one heck of a wake up call. The buildup of crusty scales from decades of softening, fudging, and outright deception fell from the eyes of the people and their king. They wept.

I can guarantee you that standing on the Gospel alone will strike a stark contrast against the world we live in today. That stand will certainly attract attention as it causes the scales to fall from the eyes of many who have allowed themselves to be deceived. No one will ever be able to confuse us with the worldly or label us as Christians in Name Only. Ironically, in our upside-down world, it is that very contrast unbelievers wield to threaten us with worldly shame should we ever obey the Holy Sprit and speak to them the Gospel of Jesus Christ. As we have already learned, this threat is a paper tiger. We have nothing to fear, for we are secure in Christ.

Imagine if every Christian in the United States stood on the *whole* Gospel every time the world contradicted God's Word. I mean every time! The folks in Washington and those who vote for them would have to answer the challenge. Since their main weapon is deceit and their battleground political, they are defenseless in the face of steadfast light and truth. That is why they will do anything, I mean *anything*, to silence the Word of God in the public square. It scares them to death when it should bring them peace. Why? Because Jesus said, "If you are not with me, you are against me. If you do not sow, you scatter" (Matthew 12:30, Luke 11:23). The light that uncompromisingly shines upon them reminds them that they are God's enemy, which means that in their current state God is against them.

They are all bark, no bite and cannot touch us spiritually. Whatever they do to us is fleetingly temporary and has no negative effect on the Gospel. This is because their response to us shows their true nature and destroys their deceitful façade. Like their father, they cannot survive without deceit. This in turn causes the Gospel to spread even more as many who have been deceived wake up to the true nature of those they follow. This has always been Satan's thorn. Every time he induces those who follow him to stamp out Christianity, it spreads.

Third, in order to stand on the *whole* Gospel, we must put on the *full armor of God*. We are not unarmed. In fact, we are armed to the teeth, according to Ephesians chapter six. Look at our incredible arsenal:

> *"6:14 Stand firm therefore having girded your loins with truth, and having put on the breastplate of righteousness,*
>
> *6:15 and having shod your feet with the preparation of the gospel of peace;*
>
> *6:16 in addition to all, taking up the shield of faith with which you will be able to extinguish all the flaming arrows of the evil one.*
>
> *6:17 And take the helmet of salvation, and the sword of the Spirit, which is the word of God."*

This is your armor. I won't walk us through all of our battle gear because I think scripture explains it much better than I can. I do want to note one element though. That last one, the "sword of the Spirit, which is the Word of God" is NOT solely a defensive weapon. Your Bible is your sword.

This tells us that the spiritual battle is not wholly defensive. You cannot gain ground by hunkering down behind castle walls. I'll let you in on a little secret. The entire earth is one contiguous spiritual battlefield. There is no bunker, no sanctuary, and no place to hide. We can only fight or surrender.

## A Distinctly Different Fight

When we fight, we use everything God has given us. Yes, Christians fight. But we do not quarrel. Paul warns us that quarrelling and bickering with the enemy only plays right into his hands (2 Timothy 2:23-26):

> "23 But refuse foolish and ignorant speculations, knowing that they produce quarrels.
> 24 The Lord's bond-servant must not be quarrelsome, but be kind to all, able to teach, patient when wronged,
> 25 with gentleness correcting those who are in opposition, if perhaps God may grant them repentance leading to the knowledge of the truth,
> 26 and they may come to their senses and escape from the snare of the devil, having been held captive by him to do his will."

We stand and fight on the strength of the Gospel and let the Holy Spirit empower us for the work we must do. We do this with kindness, a tactic that enemies of Christ would not employ. The way Christians fight confounds the enemy. That is why I speak of not meeting the unbeliever on his chosen battlefield of politics. A truly spiritual fight so befuddles him that he is often left in a sputtering rage. That's not our intention, but it does reveal to him the weakness of his ground. And that is usually the first step toward softening a hardened heart. It's a kindness heaped upon him so searing that it resembles coals upon his head. In this way, some may come to their senses.

Let me offer one example of this enormous power. If everyone who reads and shares this book corrected the error of one unbeliever (firmly and with kindness) only once each day, the magnitude of change that would subsequently sweep over this nation would astound you. Imagine!

We stand on and point to the Gospel *and nothing else*. We don't get bogged down in arguments that have only to do with man and his interpretation of "the rules." We are guided by God's love, which we hand out freely. We are not here to win individual arguments at the expense of losing the soul. We are here to win souls by the awesome power of the Holy Spirit.

Know that you are not alone. Even if no one joins you directly, know that your life-changing task is being performed throughout the country simultaneously. Fully armed defensively, you wield a sharp sword of truth that slices meat from bone. Remember the powerful promise of Hebrews 4:12-13:

> *"12 For the word of God is living and active and sharper than any two-edged sword, and piercing as far as the division of soul and spirit, of both joints and marrow, and able to judge the thoughts and intentions of the heart. 13 And there is no creature hidden from His sight, but all things are open and laid bare to the eyes of Him with whom we have to do."*

Enlist every Christian you know to stand on the Gospel. You can get on the Internet and organize both locally and nationally. You can pray for every Christian in this country to stand as one with the Father. You can pray for the lost. You can even form your own *Return of the Christian* group. On your worst day you can at least simply stand as best you can. You are not alone but one of an army of millions, led by God. If God is with us, who can stand against us? All God asks of you is that you stand for Him and *stand firm.*

# Chapter Ten

# Girding Our Loins

I was raised a Catholic, coming from a long line of San Francisco Catholics, dating back to the De Anza expedition. We altar boys did a lot of snickering over "gird your loins" when the priest would read that passage from Ephesians chapter six during Mass. Father Reagan would shoot us one of his infamous "bolt of lightning" glares whenever he would read a passage containing this phrase because our giggles, once started, could not be squelched.

One Sunday afternoon he took us aside with a wry smile on his face as he juggled a single tennis ball. We were just outside the vestibule, still in the altar boy gowns worn over our clothes. Father Reagan, who appeared to us to be about 26 feet tall, said, "Boys, I want you to tell me what is so funny about girding your loins." Tim was the first to blurt out that it sounded like Saint Paul was telling people to put on girdles. (It was the 1960s and we'd seen the commercials.) As soon as Tim spoke, I was thankful that God had led me, so I reasoned, to be an outright coward and keep my big mouth shut. But, to my surprise, Father Reagan actually crooked a half smile. He placed the tennis ball on the floor about the eighth pew down and told Tim to run down as quickly as he could, grab the tennis ball, and run back and give it to me. Then I was to do the same as a sort of relay.

Well, Tim, always the competitive one, ran like a banshee toward the tennis ball, got about a third of the way down and tripped on his gown. Down on his chest he went. He got up and ran a little more carefully, grabbed the tennis ball, tripped again as he turned around, ran headlong back toward the vestibule, and finally fell down again just before handing me the ball.

I grabbed the ball, hiked up my gown to the waist as I ran to the pew, put the ball down and ran back, easily beating Tim's time. Tim looked a bit dejected as I stood there laughing at him.

Father Reagan said something like "Go ahead and laugh, Johnny, but you're the one who just put on a girdle." It was Tim's turn to laugh. Serves me right for being a coward. So the kindly giant of a priest gathered us around and explained that girding your loins in biblical times meant gathering up your garments and tucking them in about you so that you can move quickly, efficiently, and accurately. He chided Tim for repeatedly falling down because he did not prepare himself to move effectively. And then quite off the topic, as was his nature from time to time, the priest coyly chided me for "running like a girl." I had unconsciously girded my loins. Boy, I felt like a silly girl running like that, but I sure ran faster than Tim! To me, girls were silly in those young days. Mysteriously, they became much more graceful as I got older, but now *I'm* off topic.

So we learned from Father Reagan that girding our loins, as it were, means preparing ourselves for action, tucking everything in and ensuring we are ready for anything that comes our way. We are able to move freely while skillfully avoiding any possibility of tripping up. Our beloved Father Reagan had taught us that girding ourselves with the truth allowed us to handle the adversary with a certain agility that truth brings to the task at hand. When we combine our ability to master the truth with the rest of the arsenal that is our full armor of God, we are formidable indeed.

I guess I could have shared a little early church background on this topic, but Father Reagan's example has always stuck with me as the better example. We never again snickered while he was giving the reading. We never forgot the metaphor of "girding our loins" with truth. I hope you don't either. Father Reagan has long since gone to be with the Lord, but his earthly work is still bearing fruit. I thought I would share a little of that fruit with you.

Never forget that you have no idea what will come of the seed you plant. So, my brothers and sisters in Christ, gird your loins and stand ready. All eternity, the destiny of every soul now standing against Christ, weighs in the balance of our actions. The spotlight of truth is upon us. We're on.

In, *Return of the Christian Volume II: On the March*, we will solidify our stand as we begin to take steps to retrieve lost ground.

## Afterword

# My Story and The Invitation of a Lifetime

If you are an unbeliever and have read this book from beginning to end, you are true to your word. I know that much of what I have written may have rubbed you the wrong way, but you stuck with it. That is to your credit and something everyone, no matter his or her beliefs, must respect. I would like to return the favor.

I would ask you if you might be interested in trying to understand the transformation every believer has experienced. I can't presume to know what in your history is holding you back. I'm not qualified. It's between you and God.

What I can do is share with you the miracle that is me, by the hand of Christ. I know, it sounds presumptuous, doesn't it? But I know with absolute certainty that my life is a living miracle.

It was the blood that horrified me the most. As a young child, I was forced to watch my father beat my mother to a pulp more than once. To a five-year-old, watching your mother bleed at the hands of your father is traumatic, to say the least. I was only six when, all in one day, I was forcibly and suddenly separated from my mother and two sisters forever, and dumped into a foster home of complete strangers. I can't describe the loneliness and the shock to one so young. It hurts to this day (I'm 55) to remember it. I don't want to ever feel that empty and lonely again.

After two years in a foster home, my father gained custody of me. I was glad to get out of that foster home. But I would never again be able to live with my mother because my father had falsely maligned her ability to care for me.

My father never ceased to remind me that I was stupid and that his failings with the many women he subsequently lived with were entirely due to my being so much trouble. He drank. He beat me. I mean multiple whippings on the back of my calves with the buckle end of a leather belt; once it took two people, even though they were deathly afraid of him, to pull him off of me. One of those people was his own mother. He was so strong that he could rip my pants right off of me (with my belt on) with one pull of his arm. This was the late 1960s and early 1970's when there were no child intervention programs or real child protection laws. The police never interfered inside a man's domestic household; a man's home was indeed his castle. If I told the police, and my father found out, I'd get a worse beating than the one I foolishly decided to blab about. That's how it worked in those days. But worse, my father constantly ridiculed me and smothered any hope of self-esteem. And there was always the flinching fear of another beating. He never learned to read, yet, by law, I was required to go to school. Somehow that was a serious threat to him.

We moved so often that by the time I was 15 I had attended eight schools, and I can tell you my grades weren't so great. I could never adjust and catch up before I was moved to another school. But the teachers always said I was smart, and, I admit, I was a bit of a class clown. Humor hides so much. When I was 15, my mother died unexpectedly, at age 42. I was devastated. Never again would I experience those rare moments in her loving arms. All too soon, she was gone. I didn't get to see her much, but I remember each visit and her great sense of humor. I treasure those memories to this day.

One day when I was 16, in fear of my life, I ran away from my father. After surviving several months in a juvenile detention center where they allowed me to continue high school, a great foster family took me in. I signed up for the Navy when I turned 17, and two months after I graduated high school I went straight to boot camp in San Diego. I was on my own and never looked back.

During those early years in the Navy as a cryptographer, God began to show me that maybe I wasn't so stupid after all. A scant six years after I ran away from home, I had the incredible honor of working at the highest levels of government in the White House Situation Room under President Reagan. God is truly amazing!

According to statistics I should have ended up in jail very early in life, having been consumed by a ferocious anger, if I didn't kill myself first. At the very least I should have ended up in uneducated poverty, completely dependent upon government support. I am none of those things.

Well, I *was* angry. But along the way, God sent people to me to tell me about His Son,

Jesus. Sometimes I listened, sometimes I didn't, but eventually I invited Him into my heart, to take over my life and to effectively "put His money where His mouth is." Oh, I fought Him for a long time – I was angry with Him. "What the heck kind of God allows such a thing to happen to a child?" I asked no one in particular. What perverted grand universal plan, I thought, could that possibly serve? But one very low day I had to decide if I was going to continue to go through life miserable and angry.

Being a little cocky at the time, I challenged God: Would He do what He says He'll do? During that time, as if in answer, I came to see that I wasn't so great after all but in serious peril of eternal banishment. With my sins hanging over me and mounting almost every day, that coming banishment made my time with my father look like the Cleavers from *Leave it to Beaver*. I discovered I wasn't really in a position to be so demanding of God. Graciously, my open challenge to God was not answered all at once. That is why I am so glad He sent many people my way over a period of time. He is ever so patient that way because He knows me better than I know myself. Because of that "come to Jesus" experience, I can testify first-hand to the indomitable power of a humble and honest witness.

I never would have come to Him on my own. Never. To be brutally frank in my language, God had totally pissed me off, and I did not want to have anything to do with Him. But I trusted those people who bravely came to me to bear a true witness that I could not refute. The logic and the biblical evidence they presented were infallible. But more than that, those people actually cared for me with a love that could only come from God. I had trouble understanding that at first.

And so one day I gave up trying to live life without Him. It wasn't working anyway, never had. Instead of challenging Him, I came to Him with a contrite heart and honestly asked Him to come in to my life and have His way with me. He changed my life forever. I'm not the same person I was. My anger has been gone for decades, never to reappear. I finally came to understand what that "born-again" thing is all about (John 3:3-8). He completely changes you. There is no room in a God-filled heart for anger or pride or hate. Now, man, I love everybody! I love you, and I don't even know you! I'm serious! It's a real love, not a happy, smile-all-the-time love. It's a caring, long-suffering, sacrificial love that produces a joy beyond my ability to comprehend. I'm free!

Years later, I parked outside that first foster home where I was dumped at the tender age of six. As I looked across the street at that horrible house, time melted away. I saw myself there as if it were only yesterday. I suddenly realized, through the power of the Holy Spirit that now lived in me, that through all that, Jesus had been with me. He had never left my side, even though I had not yet accepted him or even knew who the real Jesus was at the time! But now I had known Him intimately and as I sat in that car, He brought to mind exact moments in time when He had been there beside me. I discovered I was never, ever, really alone. I only know that now because after he comes into your heart, the Holy Spirit shows you these things. It's a trip and a thrill!

There is so much you don't see on the unbelieving side of the cross. Yet, there is so much evidence of Him plainly visible on that side, your side, if we choose to see it. On top of that, so many witnesses are sent to us. But Satan sows anger and pride in our hearts to blind our eyes to the obvious. I'll admit that anger feels good, I mean really good, when there is nothing left in your heart. But this most expensive deception on earth will cost you all eternity.

Now I share all this with you not to ask for your pity, or bore you to death (I hope I haven't) or to tell you how great I am. I'm not. By myself I am nothing, but with Christ I am everything.

No, instead, I want to show you the power Jesus has over any adversity. His love transcends anything we have to experience in this short life. Although I was furious with Him, He simply would not let me go. You may ask why He put me through such pain. But after you are in a personal relationship with Him, you know that the fact that He did allow it is reason enough because He is always by our side. He has never failed me and there is such joy coming for all eternity that I am actually SO GLAD he allowed me to be forged in this way.

I won't mention all the bad things I did when I was wallowing in my anger. Why? Because they are all wiped away, no longer hanging over my head. If God doesn't see them, it's because they no longer exist and I'm sure not going to go looking for them! You know, it doesn't matter what I have done or what you have done – no one is beyond His reach. A simple pivot changes you into an eternal member of His royal family.

You can stay mad at God because life has not gone your way. You can say that folks like me need a fairy tale to believe in. It's your choice to think anything you want. But I'm telling you from first-hand experience that He's real. No man-made fantasy can endure the first time you come up against real trouble. Only Christ can walk you through that fire. When I first turned to Him, I received eternal life, and I can never lose it. He proved to me that He is who he says He is. If I have to, I will die for Him even as I live for Him today.

You will never glimpse that proof you seek (if you seek it) until you strip away the veneer encasing your heart, open it up, and ask Him to come in. Oh yeah, that can be painful. But when you do, you'll see God for who He really is, and you will enjoy Him forever and ever.

I can't push, force, or cajole you into asking Him in. Honestly, I couldn't. It's not in a Christian's nature. Maybe in the past you've come up against someone who *said* he was a

*Christian* and was all over you, condemning you. There are a lot of them around. If you've read this book, you know what we say about all that. All I can do is honestly be a witness to you that it is all true. He loves you and wants you to be with Him forever. But He will never force you. A loving God, by definition, does not seek mindless robots to worship Him. He wants you to come of your own free will with a loving and contrite heart. That, my friend, is REAL, true, pure, reciprocal love, and there is nothing like it.

How do you do this? It is fantastically simple. First you have to come to Him as a child with an open and honest heart, and that does take some swallowing. I won't tell you what to pray; that's between you and Jesus. If you're stuck for words, just tell Him in your own words that you honestly want Him to come in and take control of your life. Tell Him what you have done that is wrong, even though He already knows. He wants to hear it from you. Then resolve to sin no more and to obey and love Him from this day forward. If you're sincere, He'll let you know before you do anything stupid from now on. You've confessed that you are a sinner as we all once were; you have resolved to turn from your old self and to love and obey Him the rest of your life (repent). And now ask Him in. Go for the big payday. Tell Him that you honestly believe He is the Son of God; that He died for your sins, and rose from the dead to go and prepare a place for you so that you can be with Him forever when he fulfills his promise to come again to judge the living and the dead.

Once you have accepted Christ, you will have to exercise discipline, along with the rest of us, to wait for that day, because He's coming. I wouldn't recommend delaying the inevitable. There is nothing more you need hear, nothing more you need to know. Seize the moment and make Him yours forever, before your chance is gone for good. Or, as we Baptists are fond of saying, before a Mack truck comes out of nowhere and hits you!

that's it. If you were sincere, you have just been snatched from the permanent darkness of hell that is eternal separation from God. Your slate is wiped clean, your sins to be remembered by Him no more. No one, not even Satan, can accuse you. All the things you have done no longer hang over your head as a witness against you. They were placed over His head, nailed to the cross, and He has paid the price in your place. You're not guilty anymore. You are now a Child of God, forever saved and grafted into His royal family. You're on the winning side.

Welcome! Find a good Bible-believing church, get baptized, and learn and grow in Him. When you're ready, come stand with us as we give all glory and honor to Him who has rescued us from eternal death. You, by the grace of God, are the happy ending to this book.

CPSIA information can be obtained
at www.ICGtesting.com
Printed in the USA
FFOW02n1933240116